HYMNS OF FAITH & INSPIRATION

Pamela J. Kennedy

For Josh, Doug, and Anne.
May His song always be yours.
P.J.K.

IDEALS PUBLICATIONS INCORPORATED
Nashville, Tennessee

HYMNS OF FAITH & INSPIRATION

• • • • • • • • • • • • • • • • •

ISBN 0-8249-4041-5

Text copyright ©1990 by Pamela J. Kennedy
Art copyright ©1990 by Ideals Publications Incorporated

Published by Ideals Publications Incorporated
Nashville, Tennessee

Printed and bound in the United States of America

Hymns used by permission of Broadman Press

Cover Photo
Old Lyme, Connecticut
F/Stop Pictures/Fred M. Dole

Table of Contents

HYMNS OF DEDICATION

Compelled by Love

The author of this hymn, Elizabeth Pyson Prentiss, was born in Portland, Maine, on October 26, 1818. At an early age, Elizabeth demonstrated a gift for writing both prose and poetry, and in 1834, at the age of sixteen, she became a regular contributor to the popular literary magazine, *Youth's Companion*.

After completing her formal education, Elizabeth took jobs teaching in both Massachusetts and Virginia. It was during this time in her life that she met and married Dr. George L. Prentiss, a Presbyterian minister. Elizabeth, although not a minister by profession, certainly carried on a great ministry of her own through her writings on Christian themes. One of her books, *Stepping Heavenward*, was written for young people. It outlines the techniques of living the Christian life and describes the Biblical view of the life hereafter. Shortly after its publication, this book reached sales of over 200,000 copies, earning it the reputation of a best seller.

Although Elizabeth suffered from chronically poor health, she did safely deliver three children, and considered her life at home complete and fulfilling. In 1856, however, a devastating epidemic swept New York, claiming the lives of two of her beloved children. Elizabeth was grief-stricken by the tragic loss and wrote the following poem:

I thought that prattling boys and girls
Would fill this empty room;
That my rich heart would gather flowers
From childhood's opening bloom:
One child and two green graves are mine,
This is God's gift to me;
A bleeding, fainting, broken heart,
This is my gift to Thee.

It was also during this time of deep grieving that Elizabeth found solace in the comforting hymn by Sarah Adams, "Nearer, My God, to Thee." Using an almost identical meter, she penned the verses to her well-loved hymn, "More Love to Thee." She did not intend for it to be more than a communication between herself and her Savior. She did not even show the text to her husband until thirteen years later, when he was serving as a professor at Union Theological Seminary in New York City.

Dr. Prentiss liked the hymn and encouraged his wife to publish it. That year, 1869, it was printed for the first time in a religious leaflet. The following year, "More Love to Thee" was published with music in a collection titled *Songs of Devotion,* published by W. H. Doane. It quickly gained in popularity and became a favorite hymn of dedication, used widely by preachers and teachers during the religious revival of 1870.

The philosophy expressed in the hymn's verses faithfully reflects that of its author. For despite her pain and discouragement, both physical and emotional, Elizabeth Prentiss found she could still experience great joy in expressing her love to God. Among her writings is the following reflection:

> To love Christ more is the deepest need, the constant cry of my soul . . . out in the woods, and on my bed, and out driving, when I am happy and busy, and when I am sad and idle, the whisper keeps going up for more love, more love, more love!

More Love to Thee

Elizabeth Prentiss

William H. Doane

1. More love to thee, O Christ, More love to thee! Hear thou the
2. Once earth-ly joy I craved, Sought peace and rest; Now thee a-
3. Then shall my lat-est breath Whis-per thy praise; This be the

prayer I make On bend-ed knee; This is my ear-nest plea:
lone I seek, Give what is best; This all my prayer shall be:
part-ing cry My heart shall raise; This still its prayer shall be:

More love, O Christ, to thee, More love to thee, More love to thee!

A Prayer Born in Protest

. . . .

When John Greenleaf Whittier wrote the words to this favorite American hymn, it was not with the intent that they might one day be sung in churches across the land. The five verses we sing today are actually five verses of a long poem entitled "The Brewing of Soma." In this poem, Whittier refers to the intoxicating drink, Soma, which was used in religious rites characteristic of a Hindu sect in India. The practitioners of this ritual would concoct the drink from honey and a milky sap. After drinking the Soma, they were said to have reached an ecstatic state during which they would dance and twirl, shouting and chanting in an emotional frenzy.

In 1872 there were many large revivalist meetings being held in the eastern United States. After witnessing one particularly emotional camp meeting, Whittier penned the seventeen verses of this poem, likening the meetings near his home to the Hindu rites of Soma. Both offended Whittier's Quaker temperament, as he felt it far more appropriate to seek God through the quiet inward communication of prayer and silent meditation practiced by his Quaker congregation.

Toward that end, the hymn's verses urge a quiet, simple reverence that will be responsive to the "still small voice of calm."

Whittier began his life as a poet at an early age, inspired by the works of Robert Burns. His contemporaries included such greats as Ralph Waldo Emerson, Oliver Wendell Holmes, James Russell Lowell, and Henry Wadsworth Longfellow. Unlike his well-known contemporaries, however, John Greenleaf Whittier belonged to the Quaker Society of Friends, was quite poor, and never attended a famous college or university. Indeed, his encouragement to a literary career came from a chance encounter with the editor of a weekly paper, the *Free Press*. Whittier's sister secretly sent one of her brother's poems to the editor, William Lloyd Garrison, who thought so highly of the writing that he pursued a friendship with the young man and was influential in directing him to a career in journalism. Through that avenue, Whittier traveled and reported on events and impressions from most of the great cities of the eastern United States.

After a short term in the Massachusetts legislature, Whittier returned to a career in writing, served as an editor of political writings, and worked on the staff of the newly influential magazine, *The Atlantic Monthly*. By 1866 he was a poet of national stature, and his works, both prose and poetry, were published with great success.

Dressed in his quaint Quaker garb and speaking in the distinctive style of his upbringing, Whittier was always true in lifestyle and thought to the simple philosophy of the Society of Friends. Because their worship services did not include hymns, Quakers were not known for producing great hymn writers and Whittier is reported to have said, "I am not really a hymn writer, for the very good reason that I know nothing of music. Only a few of my pieces were written for singing. A good hymn is the best use to which poetry can be devoted, but I do not claim that I have succeeded in composing one."

There are many who would argue with Whittier's modest assessment of his hymn-writing abilities. "Dear Lord and Father of Mankind" bears the stamp of its author, not only in its philosophy of a quiet faith, but in the beautiful rhythm of its poetic phrases. An appropriate tribute to this great American writer was penned by an anonymous admirer:

"John Greenleaf Whittier has left upon our literature the stamp of genius and upon religion, the touch of sanity."

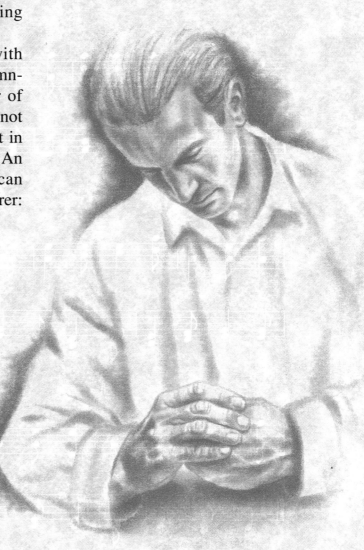

Dear Lord and Father of Mankind

JOHN GREENLEAF WHITTIER

FREDERICK C. MAKER

1. Dear Lord and Father of mankind, Forgive our foolish ways; Re-clothe us in our rightful mind; In purer lives thy service find, In deeper rev-'rence, praise.

2. Drop thy still dews of quietness, Till all our strivings cease; Take from our souls the strain and stress, And let our ordered lives confess The beauty of thy peace.

3. Breathe thro' the heats of our desire Thy coolness and thy balm; Let sense be dumb, let flesh retire; Speak thro' the earthquake, wind, and fire, O still small voice of calm!

4. In simple trust like theirs who heard, Beside the Syrian sea, The gracious calling of the Lord, Let us, like them, without a word, Rise up and follow thee. A-MEN.

Hymns of Dedication

From Fear to Faith

. . . .

Charles Wesley, the author of this well-loved hymn, was perhaps the most prolific hymn writer of all time. In all he wrote over 6,500 hymns, many of which have become an integral part of church tradition.

Born in 1707 in Lincolnshire, England, Charles Wesley was the youngest of eighteen children. His father, Samuel, was a poor country parson who made up in perseverance what he lacked in prosperity. His mother, Susannah, was a model of Christian piety and organization as she daily instructed her sizeable brood from the Bible and taught the children to sing psalms and spiritual songs as they did their chores around the house.

As a child, Charles demonstrated an unusual interest in poetry and composed verses on any subject at hand. This interest was lifelong; he is said to have often written his letters in verse. From his deathbed he even dictated one final hymn verse beginning, "In age and feebleness extreme . . . "

Despite his family's poverty, at the age of nine Charles was sent to Westminster School in London to join his older brother, John. After completing his schooling there, he continued on to Christ Church College, Oxford, where he earned his Master of Arts degree in 1730. During his years at Oxford, Charles joined with other like-minded young men to form a Christian group that became known as the "Holy Club." The club's members adhered to strict rules and methods of living, studying, and practicing their faith. Because of this, the name Methodist was later given to followers of Wesley.

In 1735, Charles Wesley was ordained a priest in the Anglican church. In this capacity, he was assigned as secretary to General Oglethorpe, the governor of the colony of Georgia in British North America. That same year, Charles traveled with the governor to North America, but he seemed unable to adjust to his situation or his occupation. In the fall of 1736, sick both in body and in soul, he set sail for England.

On this journey the ship encountered a tremendous storm, and Charles underwent a spiritual transformation. Huge waves washed over the vessel, drowning or sweeping overboard almost all of the livestock. The ship began to take on water at an alarming rate and all on board felt certain they would not survive. At this point, the captain ordered the mizzen mast be cut down in hopes of saving the ship. In Wesley's journal he records the following concerning this event: "In this dreadful moment, I bless God, I found the comfort of hope; and such joy in finding I could hope, as the world could neither give nor take away."

With his newly-found faith, Wesley sought to comfort the other passengers and "urged them to resolve, if God saved them from this distress, that they would instantly and entirely give themselves up to Him." When at last the storm ceased, the crippled vessel continued across the Atlantic, finally arriving back in England on December third. Wesley writes in his journal: "I knelt down and blessed the Hand that had conducted me through such inextricable mazes." While Wesley has not specifically indicated that it was this experience that prompted the writing of "Jesus, Lover of My Soul," one may readily see the parallels in the first two verses of the hymn.

A second life-changing experience occurred eighteen months later in May of 1738. Bedridden with fever, dysentery, and pleurisy, Wesley despaired of ever returning to health. As he lay alone in his room in Aldersgate, he had a vision of a woman named Mrs. Musgrove entering his room and telling him: "In the name of Jesus of Nazareth, arise, and believe, and thou shalt be healed of all thy infirmities." Immediately after this encounter, Charles searched the Scriptures and found verses which he felt confirmed this experience and gave him new hope. From that hour his health rapidly improved and he embarked on the intensely evangelical lifestyle for which he is remembered. His faith took on a new fervor that lost him the support of his local Anglican church, but won converts all across England, Scotland, and Wales.

It was just one year after this dramatic conversion that Charles Wesley wrote "Jesus, Lover of My Soul," and many church historians see the experience reflected in the last two verses of the hymn. Although Charles' brother John disliked the hymn for being "too sentimental," it has become one of the best known and loved hymns of Christendom and has been translated into all the languages of the missionary world.

Hymns of Dedication

Jesus, Lover of My Soul

CHARLES WESLEY   SIMEON B. MARSH

1. Je - sus, lov - er of my soul, Let me to thy bos - om fly,
2. Oth - er ref - uge have I none; Hangs my help - less soul on thee;
3. Thou, O Christ, art all I want; More than all in thee I find:
4. Plen - teous grace with thee is found, Grace to cov - er all my sin;

While the near - er wa - ters roll, While the tem - pest still is high:
Leave, O leave me not a - lone, Still sup - port and com - fort me:
Raise the fall - en, cheer the faint, Heal the sick and lead the blind:
Let the heal - ing streams a - bound; Make and keep me pure with - in:

Hide me, O my Sav - ior, hide, Till the storm of life is past;
All my trust on thee is stayed, All my help from thee I bring;
Just and ho - ly is thy name, I am all un - righteous - ness;
Thou of life the foun - tain art, Free - ly let me take of thee;

Safe in - to the ha - ven guide; O re - ceive my soul at last.
Cov - er my de - fense - less head With the shad - ow of thy wing.
False and full of sin I am, Thou art full of truth and grace.
Spring thou up with - in my heart, Rise to all e - ter - ni - ty.

A Tale of Two Sisters

. . . .

Sarah Flower Adams, the author of this well-loved hymn, was a woman of the arts. At an early age she followed her dreams of being an actress and traveled from her home in Harlow, England, to the London stage, where she played the part of Lady MacBeth in Shakespearean productions. Plagued with delicate health, however, Sarah Flower found the rigors of theatrical life exhausting, and she made a decision to channel her creative talents along literary lines. Returning home, she turned her efforts to composing poetry and prose as well as hymn texts for use by the Unitarian congregation of which she was a member. Her sister, Eliza, was an accomplished musician and composed the music for many of Sarah's verses.

In 1834, at the age of twenty-nine, Sarah married John Bridges Adams, a prominent civil engineer and inventor. Together they established a lovely home in London where they entertained a wide circle of devoted friends. Despite her increased social obligations, Sarah continued to work with her sister composing hymns. Their pastor, the Reverend William Johnson Fox, recognizing the literary and musical gifts of the two talented sisters, enlisted their aid in compiling a new hymnal for his congregation.

The project was nearing completion in 1841 when Rev. Fox lamented that he could not find a suitable hymn to use at the conclu-

sion of a sermon he was preparing on the text found in Genesis 28:10-22. In this passage, Jacob is fleeing from his home. On his journey, he stops to spend the night in the desert. Using a stone for a pillow, he falls into a deep sleep, during which he has a vivid dream. In the dream, Jacob sees a stairway or ladder extending from earth to Heaven, and with the angels of God descending and ascending upon it. Above the ladder, Jacob sees a vision of God. Waking from the dream, Jacob recommits his life to God and renames the place Bethel ("house of God").

As Rev. Fox spoke of the need to find a hymn to accompany his sermon on this text, Eliza encouraged her sister to compose a verse on the subject. Taking the challenge, Sarah sat down that day and read and reread the story of Jacob's dream. As she absorbed the details of the Bible passage, she transferred them into poetic form. When the five stanzas were completed, she had captured the essence of Jacob's dream in her hymn text. She had included the stony pillow in verse two, the angelic stairway in verse three, and the naming of the site as Bethel in verse four. Eliza wrote a melody for her sister's words and their new hymn was published in Rev. Fox's hymnal, *Hymns and Anthems*, in 1841. Three years later, "Nearer, My God, to Thee" was first sung in the United States. Although it had a cordial reception, it did not really gain much popularity until the words were set to a new melody in 1856. This melody, by which we know the hymn today, was composed by Lowell Mason, a prolific writer of church and school music.

Neither Sarah nor her sister, Eliza, lived to see the hymn gain worldwide acclaim, for within five years of its publication, both women became victims of tuberculosis.

It is a fitting tribute to them both that—as the following two stories attest—this beautiful hymn has been a comfort to men and women of faith for over 150 years.

President of the United States William McKinley lay dying from an assassin's bullet in 1901 when he was heard by his family to whisper the chorus of this favorite hymn, "Nearer, my God, to thee, nearer to thee." A few days later, at his funeral and memorial services around the country, congregations sang the hymn, remembering as they did their fallen leader.

The second story occurred as the lifeboats pulled away from the sinking *Titanic* on the night of April 14, 1912. Over 1,500 people, unable to enter lifeboats or obtain lifebelts, stood on the shuddering deck facing death. As they did so, the ship's band played this hymn and hundreds of voices rose over the roaring ocean affirming what, for them, was deep reality: "Nearer, my God, to thee, nearer to thee."

Nearer, My God, to Thee

SARAH F. ADAMS

LOWELL MASON

1. Near-er, my God, to thee, Near-er to thee! E'en tho it
2. *There let the way ap-pear, Steps un-to heav'n; All that thou
3. Then with my wak-ing tho'ts Bright with thy praise, Out of my

be a cross That rais-eth me; Still all my song shall be,
send-est me, In mer-cy giv'n; An-gels to beck-on me
ston-y griefs**Beth-el I'll raise; So by my woes to be

Near-er, my God, to thee! Near-er, my God, to thee, Near-er to thee!
Near-er, my God, to thee! Near-er, my God, to thee, Near-er to thee!
Near-er, my God, to thee! Near-er, my God, to thee, Near-er to thee! A-MEN.

Triumph through Tragedy

During the autumn of 1873, Horatio Gates Spafford and his family planned a wonderful trip to Europe to visit relatives and friends. As winter began to chill their Chicago home, Horatio, his wife Anna, and their four young daughters, Maggie, Tanetta, Annie, and Bessie (ranging in age from eighteen months to twelve years), began to anticipate the sea voyage and the reunion. When the time for the trip drew close, Spafford's business encountered some difficulties that required him to remain at home. Determined not to deprive the family of the anticipated excursion, however, he kissed his wife and daughters good-bye, bade them Godspeed, and promised to join them as soon as possible.

The Spafford women embarked on the French steamer, SS *Ville de Havre*, and began their trans-Atlantic journey. Off the coast of Newfoundland, however, tragedy struck. The ship collided with an English sailing vessel, the *Loch Earn*, ripping a gaping hole in the ship's hull. So massive was the damage that the *Ville de Havre* plunged to the bottom of the frigid sea within twenty minutes.

In the moments before the ship sank, Anna Spafford gathered her four young girls to her side and prayed with them, holding the youngest in her arms. As the icy waters of the North Atlantic swept over the decks, the three older children disappeared, and eventually even the baby was washed from her mother's embrace. Alone and near death herself, Anna was spotted from a lifeboat and plucked from the sea.

It was ten days before the survivors of the shipwreck were landed safely in Cardiff, Wales. From there Anna Spafford wired her anxious husband a brief and poignant message: "Saved alone." Boarding the next available ship, Horatio sailed to England, where he was reunited with his grieving wife.

The Spafford's close friend, evangelist Dwight L. Moody, was in Edinburgh, Scotland, at the time of the tragedy and came from there to join the bereaved couple. He later reported of that meeting that, though they were experiencing deep sorrow, the Spaffords never lost their abiding faith in God. They attested to this with their affirmation to Moody, "It is well. The will of God be done."

Returning to Chicago, Spafford rejoined his legal practice, once again becoming active in the local Presbyterian church as an elder and working with the YMCA.

A visitor to his office two years after the shipwreck remarked about the framed cable above Spafford's desk carrying only the words, "Saved alone." Retelling the tale, Spafford again affirmed, "It is well. God's will be done." He would later report that the phrase, "It is well," inspired him to formulate the words of a poem subsequently set to music by Philip P. Bliss.

With the writing of this very personal, yet universally applicable hymn, Spafford seemed to turn the focus of his energies from his law practice to the fulfillment of a life-long dream. In 1881, at the age of fifty-three, he and his wife left the United States to settle in Jerusalem. There they founded an American colony where they spent the rest of their lives.

Although Horatio Spafford's family did not live on beyond the nineteenth century, his beautiful hymn of faith lives today as a tribute to the faith of a loving Christian father. Others facing trials as great as the sea billows that swept over the sinking *Ville de Havre*, have learned to say with Spafford, "It is well with my soul."

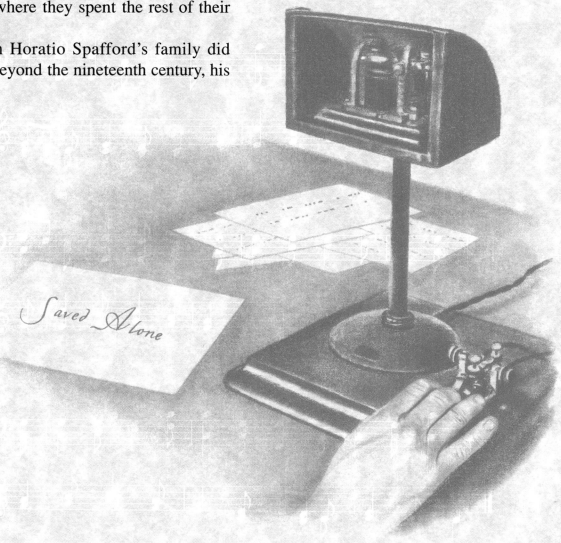

Hymns of Dedication

It Is Well with My Soul

Horatio G. Spafford

Philip P. Bliss

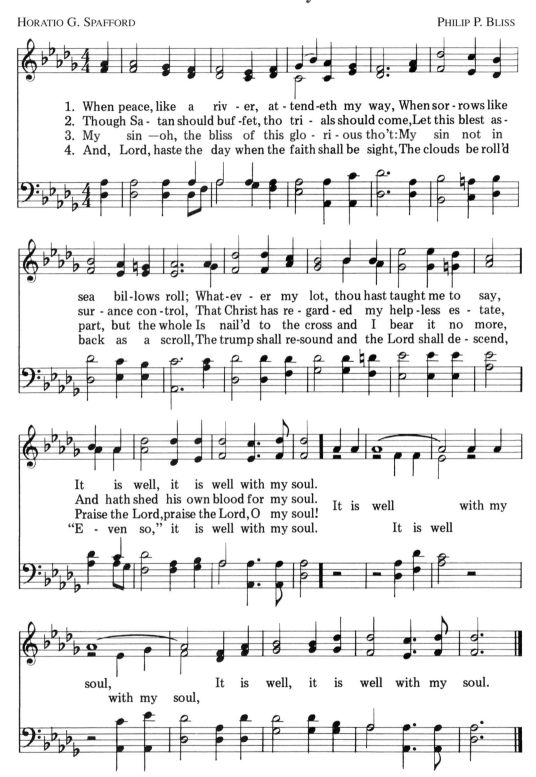

1. When peace, like a riv-er, at-tend-eth my way, When sor-rows like
2. Though Sa-tan should buf-fet, tho tri-als should come, Let this blest as-
3. My sin —oh, the bliss of this glo-ri-ous tho't: My sin not in
4. And, Lord, haste the day when the faith shall be sight, The clouds be roll'd

sea bil-lows roll; What-ev-er my lot, thou hast taught me to say,
sur-ance con-trol, That Christ has re-gard-ed my help-less es-tate,
part, but the whole Is nail'd to the cross and I bear it no more,
back as a scroll, The trump shall re-sound and the Lord shall de-scend,

It is well, it is well with my soul.
And hath shed his own blood for my soul.
Praise the Lord, praise the Lord, O my soul!
"E-ven so," it is well with my soul.

It is well   with my

It is well

soul,   It is well, it is well with my soul.

with my soul,

Hymns of Dedication

Yielded to the Hands of Their Master

delaide Pollard sat in a church prayer meeting in 1902 a depressed and discouraged Christian. Her whole life had been spent in efforts to teach the Gospel of Jesus Christ, and her heart's desire had long been to travel to Africa to minister to those who had never had an opportunity to hear such a message. Just when it seemed that things were falling into place for the accomplishment of this dream, she received word that her financial support had not been provided and that she would not be going to Africa after all.

To Adelaide, now forty years old and still single, it seemed the final blow in a lifelong string of disappointments. She had gifts of teaching and writing, but had been unable to use them in the ways she most desired. She had great dreams and ideas for ministering tirelessly for the Lord, yet her body was plagued with weakness caused by diabetes. She despaired of ever accomplishing something fulfilling and meaningful. It was at this point that she decided to attend the prayer meeting and found herself sitting beside a frail and elderly woman whom she had never seen before. As prayers were offered and requests were made for blessings, direction, and other gifts from the Lord, Adelaide sat in silence, unable to utter a prayer from her aching heart. It was then that the woman next to her offered a simple sentence that was to give Adelaide new hope. She said, "It really does not matter just what you do with us, Lord—have your way with our lives."

The words burned in Adelaide's mind. Suddenly she realized her whole life had been spent pursuing her own goals, doing what she wanted to do for God and taking little time to seek what He might have her do. As she walked home from the prayer meeting, her step had a wonderful new lightness.

Arriving home, she opened her Bible to the Old Testament book of Jeremiah. In the first four verses of the eighteenth chapter, she read these words:

> The word which came to Jeremiah from the Lord, saying arise, and go down to the potter's house, and there I will cause thee to hear my words. Then I went down to the potter's house, and, behold, he wrought a work on the wheels. And the vessel that he made of clay was marred in the hand of the potter: so he made it again another vessel, as seemed good to the potter to make it.

Adelaide saw herself as the defective pot, needing to be broken and reformed by the Master Potter after His will. As she meditated upon this thought, the words of a hymn poem began to form in her mind. Before she went to bed that night, she had composed all four verses of the popular hymn "Have Thine Own Way, Lord."

It was after this turning point in her life that Adelaide Pollard's teaching and speaking ministry took on a new dimension. She worked for several years educating missionaries at the Missionary Training School at Nyack-on-the-Hudson. She also spent time as an itinerant Bible teacher and lecturer, and she eventually did have an opportunity to go to Africa shortly before World War I. When the war broke out, however, she went to Scotland and continued her missionary efforts there. At the end of the war years, she returned to the United States and traveled extensively in the New England states, teaching the Bible despite her failing health.

On December 20, 1934, at the age of seventy-two, Adelaide Pollard died of a heart attack. True to the missionary zeal that marked her life, she was not at home in bed when this happened, but in a New York railway station, waiting to board a train for Philadelphia, where she was planning to speak.

Although she wrote other hymns, "Have Thine Own Way, Lord" is the only one still in popular use today. Perhaps that is fitting, for it was not only her philosophy of life, but her most accurate epitaph.

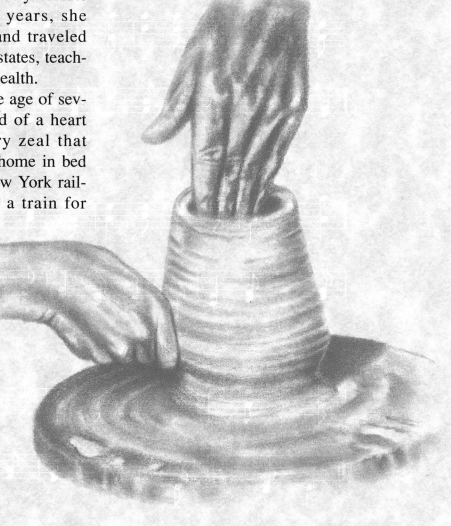

Have Thine Own Way, Lord

ADELAIDE A. POLLARD

GEORGE C. STEBBINS

1. Have thine own way, Lord! Have thine own way! Thou art the potter, I am the clay! Mold me and make me After thy will, While I am wait-ing, Yield-ed and still.

2. Have thine own way, Lord! Have thine own way! Search me and try me, Mas-ter, to-day! Whit-er than snow, Lord, Wash me just now, As in thy pres-ence Hum-bly I bow.

3. Have thine own way, Lord! Have thine own way! Wound-ed and wea-ry, Help me, I pray! Pow-er, all pow-er Sure-ly is thine! Touch me and heal me, Sav-ior di-vine.

4. Have thine own way, Lord! Have thine own way! Hold o'er my be-ing Ab-so-lute sway! Fill with thy Spir-it Till all shall see Christ on-ly, al-ways, Liv-ing in me. A-MEN.

HYMNS OF FAITH

A Chronicle of Commitment

This famous hymn of faith, with its references to those who suffered in dungeons, in chains, by fire, and by the sword, conjures images of martyrs from the time of the Roman occupation of Jerusalem to the more recent persecution of believers in today's totalitarian countries. When Frederick W. Faber penned the words of this hymn in the mid-1800s, he was specifically referring to those followers of the Roman Catholic faith who were martyred during the reign of Henry VIII when he was in the process of establishing the Anglican church in England. In fact, one of the original verses, now omitted from the hymn, reads as follows:

> Faith of our fathers! Mary's prayers
> Shall win our country back to thee;
> And through the truth that comes from God,
> England shall then indeed be free.

It is rather ironic that such words as these should come from a man like Faber at all, given his background. Frederick Faber was the son of an English clergyman who followed the teachings of Calvin with strict devotion. Raised in this environment, Faber became an early and enthusiastic proponent of the Anglican church. He graduated from Oxford University in 1843 and shortly thereafter became an Anglican minister at Elten, England.

At that time, however, the Tractarian Movement was sweeping the Church of England. Leaders of this movement held the view that deeper religious growth could only come through a return to formal worship ceremonies and liturgies of the past.

Faber joined this movement and so aligned himself with its views that he left the Anglican church after only three years of ministry and immediately joined with the Roman Catholic faith, taking the new name of Father Wilfrid.

It was shortly after this that Faber became concerned with the lack of congregational singing in the Roman Catholic church. To supply this need, Father Wilfrid began composing hymns to chronicle and honor the history of the Catholic church, especially its struggles and triumphs through the years of persecution. To that end, he composed the stirring verses of "Faith of Our Fathers."

Although originally written for a specific denomination, this hymn has become a favorite of Catholics and Protestants alike. Its verses speak of triumph over persecution and the universal ideals of liberty and freedom which appeal to men and women of all generations.

Although his life was short (he died at the age of forty-nine), Frederick Faber contributed over 150 hymns to the life of the church and was recognized for this achievement by the Pope, who granted him a Doctor of Divinity Degree.

Faith of Our Fathers

FREDERICK W. FABER

HENRI F. HEMY

1. Faith of our fa - thers! liv - ing still In spite of dun - geon,
2. Faith of our fa - thers! we will strive To win all na - tions
3. Faith of our fa - thers! we will love Both friend and foe in

fire, and sword, O how our hearts beat high with joy
un - to thee, And through the truth that comes from God
all our strife, And preach thee, too, as love knows how

When - e'er we hear that glo - rious word! Faith of our fa - thers,
Man - kind shall then be tru - ly free: Faith of our fa - thers,
By kind - ly words and vir - tuous life: Faith of our fa - thers,

ho - ly faith! We will be true to thee till death.
ho - ly faith! We will be true to thee till death.
ho - ly faith! We will be true to thee till death.

A Higher View

Many of the beautiful and best-loved hymns of faith have their beginnings in unusual circumstances or stirring events. In contrast, the author of this favorite hymn, Ray Palmer, said "My Faith Looks up to Thee" had no external occasion whatever. Even so, the life of the author and the development of the song itself are both interesting and worth review.

The son of a judge, Ray Palmer was born in Little Compton, Rhode Island, on November 12, 1808. As a youngster, Ray was a bright and earnest student who received good marks in the local public school he attended. Despite a promising academic career, however, the youngster was forced by family financial problems to quit school at the age of thirteen and take a job as a clerk in a Boston store. Overcoming his discouragement, Palmer devoted himself to his job as he had to his studies and sought personal growth and encouragement at the Park Street Congregational Church. It was there, in his teenage years, that he accepted Christ and first felt the call to become a minister of the Gospel.

Shortly after this, Palmer was able to resume his education at Andover Academy. Upon graduation, he was accepted at Yale University and received his degree from there in 1830 at the age of twenty-two. While completing his education at Yale, Palmer took a position teaching at a girls' school in New York City. He continued his teaching after graduation and it was during this time that he came to write the words to "My Faith Looks up to Thee."

As noted earlier, there was no specific event that prompted the composition of this hymn, but in his personal papers Palmer cites a time of illness and discouragement preceding the night when he sat alone in his study and penned the verses. He says:

> The words for these stanzas were born out of my own soul with very little effort. I recall that I wrote the verses with tender emotion . . . It is well-remembered that when writing the last line, 'Oh, bear me safe above, A ransomed soul!' the thought that the whole work of redemption and salvation was involved in those words, and suggested the theme of eternal praises, and this brought me to a degree of emotion that brought abundant tears.

Having written the four stanzas of the poem as a personal catharsis, Palmer copied them into the small leather-bound journal he carried, reading them over now and then for his own comfort. By his own admission he never intended to publish them or even show them to anyone else.

Two years later, however, Palmer was visiting friends in Boston and happened to meet an old acquaintance, Dr. Lowell Mason, as he walked down a busy street. Mason was a musician and composer and, at that time, was compiling a book of hymns for publication. As he and Palmer talked, he inquired if Palmer were familiar with any texts that would serve as hymns. Reaching into his own pocket, Ray Palmer produced his journal and showed Mason the poem he had written two years earlier. Mason was so impressed with the four stanzas that he accompanied Palmer into a nearby store where he copied them down. Mason took the words home and composed a tune he entitled "Olivet" to accompany them. He was so enthusiastic about the new hymn that when he again saw Palmer a few days later he proclaimed, "Mr. Palmer, you may live many years and do a good

many things, but I think you will be best known to posterity as the author of 'My Faith Looks up to Thee.'"

Ray Palmer did go on to accomplish many things in his long and fruitful life as a minister, writer, and translator of ancient Latin manuscripts. Mason's prophecy was to be reality, however, as Ray Palmer's other accomplishments have paled beside the notoriety he gained from being the author of this beloved American hymn.

My Faith Looks up to Thee

RAY PALMER

LOWELL MASON

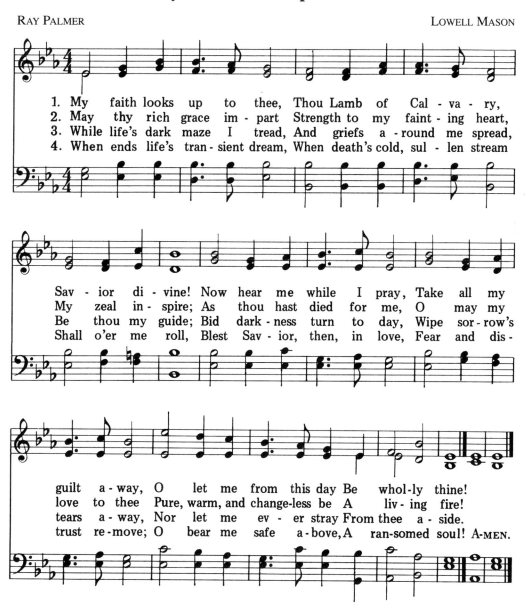

1. My faith looks up to thee, Thou Lamb of Cal - va - ry,
2. May thy rich grace im - part Strength to my faint - ing heart,
3. While life's dark maze I tread, And griefs a - round me spread,
4. When ends life's tran - sient dream, When death's cold, sul - len stream

Sav - ior di - vine! Now hear me while I pray, Take all my
My zeal in - spire; As thou hast died for me, O may my
Be thou my guide; Bid dark - ness turn to day, Wipe sor - row's
Shall o'er me roll, Blest Sav - ior, then, in love, Fear and dis -

guilt a - way, O let me from this day Be whol - ly thine!
love to thee Pure, warm, and change-less be A liv - ing fire!
tears a - way, Nor let me ev - er stray From thee a - side.
trust re - move; O bear me safe a - bove, A ran-somed soul! A-MEN.

In Search of Guidance

Although often sung at funerals, this beautiful hymn is really more appropriate for youth rallies. Its message of hope, which bursts forth in the third stanza, follows a deep desire for guidance and direction expressed in emotional terms in the first two stanzas. The circumstances of the hymn's composition are reminiscent of that seeking which typifies a young person's earnest search for God's will.

In 1833, at the age of thirty-two, John Henry Newman seemed to have all the security and status a young minister could desire. Having experienced Christian conversion at the age of fifteen, Newman had become an avid student of the Bible as a teenager. He read voraciously and was fascinated with the various church doctrines, eagerly learning from conversations with pastors and teachers as well as from reading theology. At the age of nineteen, he graduated from Oxford University and, four years later, was ordained a minister in the Church of England. From the beginning of his ministry in the church, John Newman was applauded as a charismatic speaker and teacher. Wherever he spoke, huge crowds turned out to listen. He was known as a staunch evangelical and was ruthless in his criticism of the Roman Catholic church, both in public as well as in private. To all who attended his services he appeared the picture of confident assurance.

This confident and opinionated appearance was only a facade, however; John Newman was actually embroiled in an inner turmoil that was slowly destroying both his spirit and his body. The creeds and doctrines he had so strongly embraced now seemed to him less certain and sure. He began to question the very underpinnings of his personal faith and the expression it took. His failing health and deteriorating emotional state led his friends and physician to suggest a trip to Italy where he might rest and recuperate in the warm climate and less demanding lifestyle. Agreeing with their ideas, Newman made the trip. While there, he visited Rome and made appointments with the leaders of the Catholic church to discuss his spiritual struggles.

It seemed that these conversations began the healing of his soul, but his physical health only deteriorated as he contracted deadly Sicilian fever. Almost overcome with illness and homesick after several months away from England, Newman decided to return home as soon as possible. Unfortunately, the shipping schedules didn't coincide with his plans and the only vessel heading north at that time was a boat loaded with oranges on its way to France. Nevertheless, Newman booked passage and headed for home.

His journey was long and tedious; for many days the helpless ship made little headway as it bobbed in the windless seas of the Boniface Straits between Corsica and Sar-

Hymns of Faith & Inspiration   36

dinia. As the fog rolled in to engulf the ship and its weary passenger for the third night, the disheartened Newman took pen and paper and wrote the three verses of a poem he called "The Pillar of the Cloud." The reference was to the great cloud which the Bible says God used to guide the Israelites through their wilderness experiences. In the poem, Newman pleads for God to guide him. The second verse speaks of the author's former unwillingness to follow God, but the third rings with confidence that in the future he will again be blessed with comfort as God "still will lead me on."

John Newman did regain his health and arrive safely back home in London, where he again became a great spokesman for the church. This time, however, it was the Roman Catholic church he championed and, in 1879, Pope Leo XIII made him a cardinal.

As Cardinal, Newman continued to work diligently with the church administration and was directly in charge of a large school for boys in Birmingham, England, until his death in 1890 at the age of eighty-nine.

Despite the fame he earned as a student, teacher, preacher, writer, and even as a cardinal, today John Newman is best remembered for this beautiful prayer hymn, "Lead, Kindly Light," written when his heart and soul struggled to know God's will. Those who have had a similar experience find solace and encouragement in its assuring verses.

Lead, Kindly Light

JOHN H. NEWMAN   JOHN B. DYKES

1. Lead, kind-ly Light! a-mid th'en-cir-cling gloom, Lead Thou me on;
2. I was not ev-er thus, nor prayed that Thou Shouldst lead me on;
3. So long Thy pow'r has blessed me, sure it still Will lead me on

The night is dark, and I am far from home, Lead Thou me on;
I loved to choose and see my path; but now, Lead Thou me on;
O'er moor and fen, o'er crag and tor-rent, till The night is gone;

Keep Thou my feet; I do not ask to see
I loved the gar-ish day, and spite of fears,
And with the morn those an-gel fac-es smile

The dis-tant scene; one step e-nough for me.
Pride ruled my will; Re-mem-ber not past years.
Which I have loved long since, and lost a-while! A-MEN.

Led by the Great Shepherd

. . . .

Dr. Joseph Henry Gilmore was a versatile and scholarly young man. In 1862, at the age of twenty-eight, having graduated from Brown University and Newton Theological Seminary, Gilmore was ordained as a minister in the American Baptist church. His first pastorate was at Fisherville, New Hampshire. Shortly after his ordination, Pastor Gilmore traveled to Philadelphia to visit some colleagues; and while there, he was asked to speak at a Wednesday evening prayer meeting at the First Baptist Church.

Choosing the twenty-third Psalm as his text, Gilmore spoke to the congregation about God's leadership and guidance in every area of life. As he quoted the verses of the familiar Shepherd's Psalm, he was drawn to the second and third verses which state, in part, "he leadeth me beside the still waters . . . he leadeth me in the paths of righteousness for his name's sake." After the meeting, the visiting pastor was invited home with his host, Deacon Wattson. Later that evening, as the two men continued discussing the theme of the message, Gilmore reported the following events: "During the conversation, the blessedness of God's leadership so grew upon me that I took out my pencil, wrote the hymn just as it stands today, handed it to my wife, and thought no more about it."

If the self-effacing pastor thought no more about it, he was alone. Mrs. Gilmore thought the verses had both literary and spiritual merit and submitted them without her husband's knowledge to a paper published in Boston called *The Watchman and Reflector*. When the poem was published in the paper in 1863, William Bradbury, a well-known composer of early gospel hymns, read it, liked it, and set it to music.

Two years later, in 1865, Pastor Joseph Gilmore was called to minister at the Second Baptist Church in Rochester, New York. Prior to the service, he entered the sanctuary and began thumbing through a hymnal. To his astonishment, the pages fell open to "He Leadeth Me," the hymn poem he had hastily penned three years earlier! He was not displeased, yet wondered who had written the two-line refrain with which the hymn ends: "He leadeth me, He leadeth me! By His own hand He leadeth me! His faithful follower I would be, for by His hand He leadeth me."

The mystery of the refrain was not solved until the death of the author's wife several years later. As he went through her papers, Gilmore came upon his own handwritten text of "He Leadeth Me." There, clearly penned in his own writing, was the two-line refrain. It would seem that the title of Gilmore's poem was more prophetic than even he had realized!

After the publication and popularity of this first hymn, Gilmore went on to attain success as a lecturer, university teacher, textbook writer, and preacher; but his memory is kept alive today by none of these achievements. A small bronze plaque placed in the cornerstone of the office building that now stands on the site of the First Baptist Church in Philadelphia remains his public memorial. Below the words of the hymn's first stanza, the inscription reads: "In recognition of the beauty and fame of this beloved hymn, and in remembrance of its distinguished author."

He Leadeth Me!

Joseph H. Gilmore

William B. Bradbury

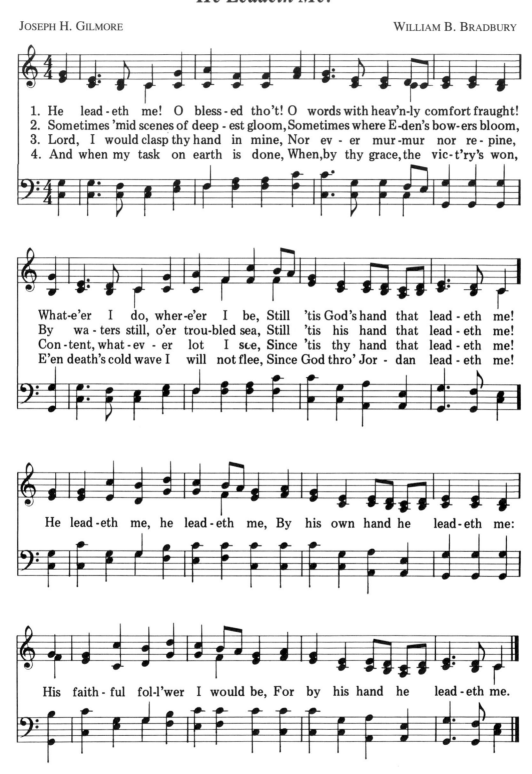

1. He lead-eth me! O bless-ed tho't! O words with heav'n-ly comfort fraught!
2. Sometimes 'mid scenes of deep - est gloom, Sometimes where E-den's bow-ers bloom,
3. Lord, I would clasp thy hand in mine, Nor ev - er mur-mur nor re - pine,
4. And when my task on earth is done, When, by thy grace, the vic-t'ry's won,

What-e'er I do, wher-e'er I be, Still 'tis God's hand that lead-eth me!
By wa - ters still, o'er trou-bled sea, Still 'tis his hand that lead-eth me!
Con-tent, what-ev - er lot I see, Since 'tis thy hand that lead-eth me!
E'en death's cold wave I will not flee, Since God thro' Jor - dan lead-eth me!

He lead-eth me, he lead-eth me, By his own hand he lead-eth me:

His faith-ful fol-l'wer I would be, For by his hand he lead-eth me.

Focused on Faith

When Helen Lemmel was only twelve years old, her family moved from England to America. Her father was a Wesleyan Methodist pastor determined to strike out in a new area of ministry. After a brief time in Mississippi, he moved his family to Wisconsin, where they settled.

Even at this young age, Helen showed remarkable musical gifts and her parents saw to it that she received voice lessons from the finest teachers. After she had finished school, Helen traveled to Germany for further vocal training and studied there for four years. Returning to Wisconsin, Lemmel launched a ministry of her own, giving concerts in auditoriums and churches across the Midwest. She was also a member of a women's quartet that traveled on the Chautauqua Circuit, bringing concerts to small rural towns and villages that would otherwise have no opportunities to hear quality performers.

Although talented enough to succeed as a professional singer, Helen Lemmel sought fulfillment using her musical gifts as a form of ministry to God. She joined the faculty of the Moody Bible Institute, teaching vocal music. She served in this capacity at both their Chicago and Los Angeles campuses.

It was in the year 1918, when she was fifty-four years old, that Helen Lemmel wrote the beautiful and challenging hymn, "Turn Your Eyes upon Jesus." She had been visiting with a missionary friend who had shared with her a gospel tract by Lillias Trotter, titled "Focused." The pamphlet included the statement: "So then, turn your eyes upon Him, look full into His face and you will find that the things of earth will acquire a strange new dimness." The words seemed to repeat themselves over and over in her mind during the following week. In her memoirs she reports the following:

> Suddenly, as if commanded to stop and listen, I stood still, and singing in my soul and spirit was the chorus, with not one conscious moment of putting word to word to make rhyme, or note to note to make melody. The verses were written the same week, after the usual manner of composition, but nonetheless dictated by the Holy Spirit.

The song was published in 1922 by the British National Sunday School Union in a the book called *Glad Songs*, which contained sixty-six other songs by Helen Lemmel and was used extensively by the Keswick Bible Conference. It was at this conference that "Turn Your Eyes upon Jesus" first gained popularity as a hymn of invitation and dedication to the life of a deeper commitment to Christ.

Two years later, the hymn was first published in the United States and has since been included in most evangelical hymnals.

Although she is perhaps best known for having written this favorite hymn, it was only one of over 500 hymns to come from her pen. In addition to her reputation as a prolific hymn writer, Mrs. Lemmel is well-known in musical circles for her contributions in the field of children's music. A gifted writer as well, she composed and published several works of poetry and authored a popular book for children entitled *Story of the Bible*.

In her later years, Helen Lemmel settled in the Pacific Northwest, making her home in Seattle, Washington, where she became an active member of the Ballard Baptist Church. It would seem that she made the words of her hymn her personal creed as she continually turned her eyes toward Jesus, serving him faithfully until the day of her death, November 1, 1961, at the age of ninety-six.

Turn Your Eyes upon Jesus

HELEN H. LEMMEL   HELEN H. LEMMEL

1. O soul, are you wea-ry and trou-bled? No light in the
2. Thro' death in-to life ev-er-last-ing He passed, and we
3. His word shall not fail you—he prom-ised; Be-lieve him, and

dark-ness you see? There's light for a look at the Sav-ior, And
fol-low him there; O-ver us sin no more hath do-min-ion—For
all will be well: Then go to a world that is dy-ing, His

life more a-bun-dant and free!
more than con-q'rors we are! Turn your eyes up-on Je-sus,
per-fect sal-va-tion to tell!

Look full in his won-der-ful face, And the things of

earth will grow strange-ly dim In the light of his glo-ry and grace.

A Stone of Contention

While many of our favorite hymns can boast of being written in moments of great inspiration or in times of life-changing crises, very few can trace their origins to an angry theological battle. "Rock of Ages," by Augustus Toplady, however, was the product of just such a rancorous debate.

In the early 1770s, great theological arguments raged in England between the followers of John and Charles Wesley and those of John Calvin. Early in his pastoral career, Augustus Montague Toplady, an ordained minister in the Anglican church, was attracted to the teachings of the Wesley brothers. As time went on, however, Toplady found himself at philosophical odds over the Wesleyan doctrine of sanctification. This doctrine stated, in part, that it was possible for a truly devout believer to attain a state of heavenly perfection here on earth and thus live without consciously sinning. On the contrary, Toplady believed, along with the followers of John Calvin, that only through the grace of God, and on no amount of human effort or good intention, could one ever become justified to God.

In public debates, religious pamphlets, sermons, and angry letters, Wesley and Toplady did theological battle. As a final salvo in his attack on Wesley, in an essay published in 1776 in *The Gospel Magazine,* Toplady published the hymn text we know today as "Rock of Ages." It is interesting to note that the poem included lines in direct contradiction of Wesley's theology: "Could my tears forever flow, could my zeal no languor know, these for sin could not atone—Thou must save, and Thou alone."

So intent was Toplady upon making the poem as personal an attack on Charles Wesley as possible that he used many of Wesley's own figures of speech in writing "Rock of Ages." In a hymn of his own, Wesley had described Jesus Christ as a "Rock struck for me" and had continued, "let those two streams of Blood and Water which once gushed out of Thy side bring down Pardon and Holiness into my soul."

Although the first two verses seem a well-aimed rebuttal at Wesleyan theology, the third can be seen to be a very personal affirmation of Toplady's faith. Having lived most of his life in poor health, he was, at the time of the hymn's composition, suffering from tuberculosis. Within two years, in 1778, he died, at the age of thirty-eight. It is ironic that a hymn born out of such dissension and controversy would have brought such peace and hope to Christians over the past two centuries.

Perhaps it is for this very reason that about eight years after "Rock of Ages" was written, a new and very different story of its origins began to circulate. Apparently wishing to gain fame, and maybe a bit of mystical propriety, the vicar of Blagdon—Toplady's former parish—told the following lovely, but inaccurate, tale:

As young Augustus Toplady, curate of Blagdon in Somerset, England, strode about the rocky countryside one Sunday afternoon in 1776, he saw dark storm clouds gathering. As the sky became increasingly threatening and thunder rolled over the rocky promentaries of Burrington Combe, the anxious pastor searched for a place of safety from the coming storm. Spying a small ledge between towering boulders, Toplady crept under the sheltering rocks and crouched in their mighty shadows while the storm raged. While the wind roared and the thunder crashed, the words of the beloved hymn came unbidden to his mind; and taking a scrap of paper from his pocket, he hastily scrawled the inspired verses.

Visitors to Burrington Combe today are still directed to view the towering rocks and told this romantic tale. And one wonders if Toplady would mind so much, given the comfort and security his stirring words have provided over the years.

Rock of Ages

AUGUSTUS M. TOPLADY

THOMAS HASTINGS

1. Rock of A - ges, cleft for me, Let me hide my - self in thee;
2. Not the la - bors of my hands Can ful - fill thy law's de - mands;
3. While I draw this fleet - ing breath, When mine eyes shall close in death,

Let the wa - ter and the blood, From thy wound - ed side which flowed,
Could my zeal no res - pite know, Could my tears for - ev - er flow,
When I rise to worlds un - known, And be - hold thee on thy throne,

Be of sin the dou - ble cure, Save from wrath and make me pure.
All for sin could not a - tone; Thou must save, and thou a - lone.
Rock of A - ges, cleft for me, Let me hide my - self in thee. A - MEN.

HYMNS OF PRAISE

A Greatness without Boundaries

This well-loved hymn, made famous by the Billy Graham crusades and George Beverly Shea in particular, has one of the most fascinating histories of any modern hymn. It was written in different countries and diverse languages over the course of seventy years with the input of several translators who never met!

The life of this majestic hymn of praise began in 1886 on a picturesque estate on the southern coast of Sweden. The Reverend Carl Boberg, who was also a member of the Swedish parliament and a successful editor, strolled across the well-kept grounds of the coastal estate and, as he did so, was caught in a sudden summer thunderstorm. Taking cover under some trees, he watched as the sky changed from angry blacks and grays streaked with flashes of lightning to clear, bright blue again. In the stillness after the storm, Boberg heard the birds begin to sing.

Boberg reported that witnessing this awesome demonstration of the variety and power of God caused him to fall to his knees in a spontaneous outburst of adoration and praise. After returning home, he put his thoughts on paper in a poem he titled "O Store Gud" (O Great God). This poem was later published in several periodicals, including the one Boberg edited, paired with a Swedish folk melody.

In 1907, Manfred von Glehn, a German residing in Estonia, saw the hymn and translated it into his native tongue. Five years later, in 1912, a Russian pastor, Rev. Ivan S. Prokhanoff, well-known for his evangelical zeal and his efforts to bring fresh expressions of faith into the church, came across the German version and translated it into Russian for his congregations. Prokhanoff printed several small booklets of hymns; and, in 1922, his friends in the American Bible Society had all his hymns compiled into one volume and published the Russian hymnal in New York. Copies were then shipped back to Russia for use in the various Christian churches there.

It was at this time that the hymn fell into the hands of Mr. and Mrs. Stuart K. Hine, an English couple serving as missionaries in the Ukraine. Initially, the Hines used the Russian version exclusively in their ministry, but as they traveled through the countryside, singing the hymn as a duet, they were impressed with the effect it had on those who had never heard the Gospel before. It was during this time that the idea of an English translation came to Stuart Hine. Although he used many of the same phrases written by Boberg decades earlier, Hine also included impressions of God's grandeur gained from his excursions in the Carpathian mountains, where he had witnessed "all the works Thy hands have made." In addition, he recalled the miracle of the Gospel and the gift of salvation offered in Jesus Christ, and the effects of this on the unevangelized villages in Russia, Poland, Czechoslovakia, and Romania.

With these recent memories in his thoughts, Hine wrote the English translation of the first three verses of "How Great Thou Art."

When war broke out in 1939, the Hines were forced to leave their missionary posts in Eastern Europe and return to Great Britain. Among their personal belongings were the three stanzas of the hymn. Although they had been forced to leave their foreign field, the Hines continued to minister to the flood of refugees that streamed into Britain. Stuart Hine later reported that it was the repeated question of these displaced persons, "When will we be going home?" that caused him to write the fourth stanza of the hymn, recalling that final home-going of all believers.

In 1949, Stuart Hine published his hymn, "How Great Thou Art," in a Russian gospel magazine and missionaries from all over the world requested reprints. It was one of these reprinted leaflets that was handed to a member of a Billy Graham crusade team in 1954. The hymn was included in the Toronto, Canada, crusade in 1955 and has been a favorite of Graham's crusade audiences ever since. Its great popularity can be attributed not only to the beautiful words and uplifting melody, but also to the continual exposure the hymn received on radio and television broadcasts in the last thirty years.

"How Great Thou Art" is a hymn that begins on earth, and ends in heaven, carrying the worshipper from the creation with all its beauty and splendor, to the Creator in all His majesty. It is this uplifting quality of both message and music that has made this hymn a favorite of congregations all around the world.

How Great Thou Art

STUART K. HINE

1. O Lord my God! When I in awe-some won-der Con-sid-er all the *worlds thy hands have made, I see the stars, I hear the *roll-ing thun-der, Thy pow'r thro'-out the u-ni-verse dis-played,

2. When thro' the woods and for-est glades I wan-der, And hear the birds sing sweet-ly in the trees; When I look down from loft-y moun-tain gran-deur, And hear the brook and feel the gen-tle breeze;

3. And when I think that God, his Son not spar-ing, Sent him to die, I scarce can take it in; That on the cross, my bur-den glad-ly bear-ing, He bled and died to take a-way my sin;

4. When Christ shall come with shout of ac-cla-ma-tion, And take me home, what joy shall fill my heart! Then I shall bow in hum-ble ad-o-ra-tion, And there pro-claim, my God, how great thou art!

Then sings my soul, my Sav-ior God to thee; How great thou art, how great thou art! Then sings my soul, my Sav-ior God to thee; How great thou art, how great thou art!

Tribute to the Trinity

The Trinity, God in three persons, is a central doctrine of the Christian faith, clearly stated for the first time at the council of Nicaea in 325 A.D. Scriptural support for this doctrine is found in several places, but perhaps most clearly in two passages which repeat the phrase "holy, holy, holy" and imply a threefold subject of angelic worship. The first passage is from the Old Testament book of Isaiah, chapter six, verse three: "Holy, holy, holy, is the Lord of hosts; the whole earth is full of his glory." The second passage is found in the New Testament book of Revelation, chapter 4, verse 8: "Holy, holy, holy, Lord God Almighty, who was and is and is to come." It was to this last passage that Reginald Heber turned when he wanted to write a hymn for Trinity Sunday, to be sung by his congregation of the parish at Hodnet in western England. He served as vicar at the church there from 1807 until 1823, and during his tenure was known as a prolific writer of poetry, essays, and hymns.

Born into a wealthy and well-educated family on April 21, 1783, Reginald Heber was raised in an atmosphere of scholarly pursuits. When he was seventeen, he traveled to Oxford University where he distinguished himself early on for his literary abilities. In his first year at Oxford, he won a prize for the best Latin poem; in his second year, he was awarded the coveted Newgate Prize for his English poem entitled "Palestine." In 1807 at the age of twenty-four, Heber was ordained a priest in the Church of England and began his ministry in the small parish at Hodnet.

Throughout his sixteen years at Hodnet, Heber composed hymns of uncommon lyric beauty, reflecting the Romantic Movement sweeping Europe at that time. Lord Tennyson, one of Heber's contemporaries, was said to have praised "Holy, Holy, Holy" as the greatest poetic hymn in the English language. This was high praise indeed, coming from one of history's greatest poets.

Looking carefully at the hymn, one finds it not only speaks of the Trinity, but also speaks *in* trinities. Verse one contains a trinity of characteristics—holy, merciful, and mighty. Verse two includes a trinity of time—wert, art, and evermore shall be. Verse three contains another trinity of characteristics—power, love, and purity, and the fourth verse concludes in a trinity defining the scope of God's control—earth, sky, and sea. Heber's attempt to clarify the Trinity for his small nineteenth century parishoners has become a classic hymn of worship for Christians ever since and is sung in churches of almost all denominations.

Despite his fulfilling ministry in his church, Heber longed to serve in the mission field. In 1823, when he was forty years old, his dreams were realized. He was asked to take the post of the Bishop of Calcutta. Moving from England to the tropical climate of India, Heber threw himself into his work, traveling across the country tirelessly to advance the cause of the church. He was especially distressed by the strict caste system in the country and spoke out against it at every opportunity.

On Sunday morning, April 3rd, 1826, the English Bishop of Calcutta again stood before a crowd of Indian citizens decrying the evils of the caste system. It was an extremely hot and humid day and Heber was exhausted at the close of his sermon. Thankfully, he accepted the invitation of his host in the city of Trichinopoly to cool off in the family swimming pool. It was there that Reginald Heber was discovered later in the day, drowned, the apparent victim of a stroke.

Mourned by friends and family, Heber was buried at the Anglican church in Trichinopoly. His inspiration, however, lived on in a book of fifty-seven hymns which were collected and published by his widow the following year. Most of these lovely hymns are still in use today. Although his life was relatively short, it has influenced believers throughout the century following his death and there is no doubt that as long as Christians sing, they will raise their voices in Heber's beautiful hymn of worship, "Holy, Holy, Holy."

Holy, Holy, Holy

REGINALD HEBER

JOHN B. DYKES

1. Ho - ly, ho - ly, ho - ly! Lord God Al - might - y!
2. Ho - ly, ho - ly, ho - ly! all the saints a - dore thee,
3. Ho - ly, ho - ly, ho - ly! tho the dark - ness hide thee,
4. Ho - ly, ho - ly, ho - ly! Lord God Al - might - y!

Ear - ly in the morn - ing our song shall rise to thee;
Cast - ing down their gold - en crowns a - round the glass - y sea;
Tho the eye of sin - ful man thy glo - ry may not see;
All thy works shall praise thy name, in earth, and sky, and sea;

Ho - ly, ho - ly, ho - ly, mer - ci - ful and might - y!
Cher - u - bim and ser - a - phim fall - ing down be - fore thee,
On - ly thou art ho - ly; there is none be - side thee,
Ho - ly, ho - ly, ho - ly; mer - ci - ful and might - y!

God in three Per - sons, bless - ed Trin - i - ty!
Who wert, and art, and ev - er - more shalt be.
Per - fect in pow'r, in love, and pu - ri - ty.
God in three Per - sons bless - ed Trin - i - ty! A - MEN.

A Pauper's Prayer

• •

One of the most fascinating figures in church history is Giovanni Bernardone, better known in Christendom as St. Francis of Assisi. Born in 1182 in the Italian hill town of Assisi, Giovanni was the son of a wealthy cloth merchant. His youth was characterized by a carefree, happy personality, a sparkling wit, and an inclination toward mischief. He loved to sing and compose bawdy poetry, to run with his gang of undisciplined friends, and to party in the Italian taverns near his home.

One night, as he partied at a banquet given for several of his companions, Giovanni was struck by their self-indulgence. He became pensive and so quiet that his companions first questioned him, then, when they could get no answer, accused him of being deep in thought over the prospect of getting married. It is reported that Giovanni replied, "Yes, I am thinking of taking a wife more beautiful, more rich, more pure than you could ever imagine. Her name is Lady Poverty." Shortly after this incident, he was praying in a ruined hermitage of St. Damian outside his hometown when he had a very personal and miraculous encounter with Christ. Giovanni said that at this time, Jesus spoke to him from the crucifix, accepted him as a servant, and won his undying devotion.

Taking the new name of Francis, he renounced his former lifestyle and comrades and dedicated himself to traveling around the Italian countryside, preaching the love of Jesus, and enlisting people to help rebuild ruined shrines. Although disowned by his wealthy father, Francis soon gathered a group of like-minded young men to his cause; together they worked and preached among the sick and poor. When their group reached twelve in number, Francis led them on a pilgrimage to Rome to request recognition from Pope Innocent III. At first, the Pope refused the request; but after dreaming about Francis, he reconsidered. In 1210, the Pope blessed and established the movement that came to be known as the Franciscans.

With the blessings of the church, Francis and his band of followers traveled across the Mediterranean lands for fourteen years. Their message was one of hope and peace, but also one of practicalities. He emphasized three specific ways in which believers should prove their true conversion: giving up all ill-gotten gains, renouncing their hatreds, and reconciling with former enemies. Francis attempted through his lifestyle to be the model of honesty and love of Jesus for all men of all social situations. As the movement grew, there were conflicts from within and without the religious community, but Francis never gave up his simple devotion to preaching the love and joy of a life dedicated to God.

Francis was well-known for his love of nature and the wonders of the universe, and also for his respect for the creatures of the animal kingdom. He often referred to them as

Hymns of Praise

"brother" and "sister," and there are many legends that speak of his ability to understand and to be understood by the animals.

After almost fifteen years of itinerant preaching, Francis of Assisi was weak and ill. His eyesight was failing and he was experiencing extreme loneliness and even depression. His order of Franciscans had grown so large that he had lost control, and rules and regulations were adopted that were far from his original intent. Disappointed and desperately in need of quiet and comfort, Francis traveled to the Convent of St. Damian. He wanted to say farewell to Sister Clara, the first woman who, years before, responded to his call to Lady Poverty and began the Sisters of his order. Francis and Clara shared a deep respect and devotion to God as well as to each other. When she saw his grave condition, she insisted he stay at the convent. She and the sisters prepared a tiny cell for him in the garden, constructed of reeds and grasses, a place where he could rest and be undisturbed.

By day, the nearly blind Francis lay on the ground, meditating and praying in the little hut. By night, an army of mice and rats invaded his solitude, climbing about over his bed and even his face, keeping him awake. Despite the hardships of the situation, Francis began to regain his strength; the Sisters soon heard him singing as they went about their daily tasks. He took his meals in the Convent and spent many hours deep in conversation with Clara.

It was after one of these times of shared insight that Francis composed his famous "Canticle of the Sun." In its seven stanzas Francis praises God for all His creatures, especially the sun, moon, wind, earth, and all those who love and pardon one another. It was a beautiful summary of the faith of this devoted disciple of Christ who went to live with his Lord only one year later. Within two years after his death, Francis was canonized by the Catholic church as St. Francis of Assisi.

The English translation of "Canticle of the Sun" was made by an English rector, William Draper, as he searched for a hymn to be used in a children's choir festival. He named the hymn "All Creatures of Our God and King." Since that time it has been sung and enjoyed in churches and Sunday schools across the world.

Faith under Fire

．．．

The lovely words of praise and faith found in this hymn would lead us to believe that they were forged at a time of great victory. In reality, the opposite is true. Martin Rinkart, a Lutheran minister in Eilenburg, Germany, wrote this uplifting hymn in the midst of his country's darkest moments.

After a childhood spent in the home of his father, a poor coppersmith, Martin Rinkart found an outlet for his skills as a singer and composer as a chorister in the well-known St. Thomas Church of Leipzig, Germany. While there, he worked his way through the University of Leipzig until he attained his degree and was ordained, at the age of thirty-one, as a minister in the Lutheran church. The year was 1617 and the religious turmoil that was born in the Protestant Reformation was sweeping across the European continent. Wars broke out and for the next thirty years, would rage throughout the German cities and countryside.

Upon his ordination, Rev. Martin Rinkart was assigned as minister in his hometown of Eilenburg. A walled city, Eilenburg was looked upon as a place of refuge and safety for those thousands of refugees fleeing the attacks of the warring armies during the Thirty Years' War. Overcrowded and under-supplied with food, sanitary facilities, and medical care, the walled city became, instead, a city of death. Plagues and pestilence raged through the crowded streets and homes, claiming hundreds of victims. All during the three decades of devastation, Rinkart was a model to his weak and weary parishoners. He faithfully tended them, encouraged them, and even entertained them with plays depicting different aspects of the Protestant Reformation. In the midst of their constant pain and suffering, he composed over sixty hymns of faith and hope, turning the eyes of his people from their own despair to the power and love of God. He encouraged them to see that their circumstances were temporary, while God's blessings were eternal, transcending earth's difficulties. It was this confidence that allowed Rinkart to continue in his ministry to the sick and dying of Eilenburg, even through the terrible plague of 1637. The other pastors had died or fled and Rinkart was left alone to bury close to 4,500 men, women, and children, sometimes conducting up to forty-five funerals a day. During this sad and depressing time, he even buried his beloved wife.

As the years of war drew to a close, several armies overran the walled city, exacting services and tribute from the impoverished population. At one point, a Swedish army occupied Eilenburg and the general demanded the citizens pay a large sum of money in tribute. On behalf of Eilenburg's destitute townspeople, Rev. Rinkart spoke to the general, begging for a reduction since there was no way the levy could be paid. The general was angry and unmoved by Rinkart's pleas. Facing possible death, Rinkart turned to his assembled companions and instructed them to kneel with the following injunction: "Come, my children, we can find no mercy with man; let us take refuge with God." He then led them in prayer and in the singing of a familiar hymn. Stunned, the Swedish general watched the dramatic demonstration of faith and courage in silence. When Rinkart rose from his knees, the general instructed that the levy be reduced, and he spared the city any further trouble.

It was out of this faith in God's providence despite difficulties that Martin Rinkart drew the beliefs expressed in his beloved hymn, "Now Thank We All Our God." He had learned, like the apostle Paul, that nothing in life or death could separate him from the love of God he found through Jesus Christ.

Hymns of Praise

Now Thank We All Our God

MARTIN RINKART

JOHANN CRUGER

1. Now thank we all our God With heart and hands and voic- es,
2. O may this boun-teous God Thro' all our life be near us,
3. All praise and thanks to God The Fa - ther now be giv- en,

Who won-drous things hath done, In whom his world re - joic - es;
With ev - er joy - ful hearts And bless - ed peace to cheer us;
The Son, and him who reigns With them in high - est heav - en,

Who, from our moth-er's arms, Hath blest us on our way
And keep us in his grace, And guide us when per - plexed,
The one e - ter - nal God, Whom earth and heav'n a - dore;

With count-less gifts of love, And still is ours to - day.
And free us from all ills In this world and the next.
For thus it was, is now, And shall be ev - er - more. A - MEN.

A Pastor Honors His King

· ·

Edward Perronet was born in 1726 in the English town of Sundridge. The son of a well-known and respected vicar in the Church of England, young Edward grew up in and around the parish church. Early on he demonstrated an interest in religious matters, and when his father, Vincent, was visited by traveling evangelists, Edward would sit and listen intently to their conversations.

As the evangelical movement headed by John and Charles Wesley swept across the English countryside, the elder Perronet became a trusted counselor to the younger preachers. Often John Wesley would ride up to the parish on horseback, anxious to discuss with the vicar some matter of doctrine or administration. It was during these visits that Edward developed an admiration for the daring Wesley and his determined efforts to break from the traditional forms of the Anglican church. Just as young Timothy in New Testament times left home to follow his hero, Paul, Edward Perronet broke with his traditionalist background and cast his lot with the Wesleys.

If it was adventure he sought, he was not to be disappointed, for shortly after his association with John Wesley, Perronet was involved in incidents of persecution where, according to Wesley's diary: "he was thrown down and rolled in mud and mire. Stones were hurled and windows broken."

Despite this persecution, Perronet continued as a faithful disciple of Wesley, being present with the evangelist at virtually all of his preaching meetings. Inspired by his mentor, Edward also began to preach, but determined never to do so in the presence of John Wesley. Wesley, eighteen years his senior, felt the young man needed to overcome this fear and decided to force the issue. Before a large congregation one Sunday morning, John Wesley smiled down at this young friend then dramatically announced to the waiting parishioners that the following day they would be treated to a wonderful message from young Edward Perronet!

Perronet was dumbstruck—and not a little irritated that Wesley would put him in such an uncomfortable position. He did not wish to cause public embarrassment by refusing the evangelist's request, but neither did he feel prepared or inclined to present the next day's sermon. In the end, Perronet's will and determination brought to mind the solution to his dilemma. In the morning he mounted the pulpit, smiled confidently at Wesley and the eager congregation, and then announced: "Although I have no sermon of my own to give to you, I promise you I shall deliver the finest one ever heard." He then opened his Bible and proceeded to read the Sermon on the Mount, word for word. When he completed the reading, he closed the book, smiled and took his seat without comment.

Perhaps it was this indelible streak of independence that finally led Perronet to break with the Wesleys several years later over the issue of evangelists administering the sacraments. Whatever the reason, Edward Perronet left the Wesleys and became the pastor of an independent church at Canterbury, England. As he pastored his little flock of country folk, Perronet saw the need for new and inspiring hymns. Using his abundant gifts as a writer, he wrote three small volumes of hymns, published in 1756, 1782, and 1785. "All Hail the Power of Jesus' Name" was included in the second volume, having been previously published alone in a 1779 issue of *Gospel Magazine*.

The hymn affirms Perronet's conviction that God ought always to be worshipped in great glory and honor, with an emphasis upon his holy kingship. Paired with a beautiful melody written by Edward Shrubsole, the hymn became popular with congregations across England. When the text was first intro-duced in America, however, a self-taught Massachusetts carpenter composed the tune, "Coronation," for the stirring words and it is to this tune that the hymn is best known in the United States.

The majestic words of Perronet's hymn have inspired Christians around the world for the past two centuries with an appeal that touches the hearts of those from every walk of life. Missionaries have related how groups of unlearned tribesmen were moved to tears by the hymn's proclamation, and it is said that whenever Queen Victoria had the hymn played, she would direct that her jeweled crown be removed in deference to the hymn's message that Jesus should be crowned Lord of all!

All Hail the Power of Jesus' Name

EDWARD PERRONET   JAMES ELLOR

1. All hail the pow'r of Je - sus' name! Let an - gels pros-trate fall;
2. Ye cho - sen seed of Is - rael's race, Ye ran-somed from the fall,
3. Let ev - 'ry kin - dred, ev - 'ry tribe, On this ter - res - trial ball,
4. O that with yon - der sa - cred throng We at his feet may fall!

Bring forth the roy - al di - a - dem,
Hail him who saves you by his grace,
To him all maj - es - ty as - cribe,
We'll join the ev - er - last - ing song,

And crown him Lord of all; Bring forth the roy - al
And crown him Lord of all; Hail him who saves you
And crown him Lord of all; To him all maj - es -
And crown him Lord of all; We'll join the ev - er -

di - a - dem, And crown him Lord of all.
by his grace, And crown him Lord of all.
ty as - cribe, And crown him Lord of all.
last - ing song, And crown him Lord of all. A - MEN.

Chords of Coincidence

This hymn, often used in communion services, was the result of some very interesting coincidences that took place in the Monument Street Methodist Church of Baltimore, Maryland, in the spring of 1865.

The church's cabinet organ had been moved to the home of the organist, Thomas Grape, while the church was undergoing some remodeling. Since he had access to the organ all the time, Grape spent many hours sitting at the keyboard practicing and composing. He was trying to write a tune for a hymn composed by William Bradbury and finally came up with one that satisfied him. He entitled the melody he had written, "All to Christ I Owe" and gave it to the pastor of the Monument Street Church, Rev. George Schrick. Rev. Schrick did not feel that Grape's music was quite right for Bradbury's poem, and he tucked it away in his files.

Elvina Mabel Hall was a member of the choir at the same church where Thomas Grape was organist. She and her husband had been faithful members there for many years and she loved being part of the choir and singing the lovely hymns and anthems each week. One Sunday morning in the spring of 1865, Elvina's attention drifted from the Reverend Schrick's sermon. She began to think about the pastor's words regarding God's forgiveness and all that Christ had done to provide redemption for mankind, but specifically for her. As she meditated on this, she became more and more filled with gratitude and she felt a compulsion to put her thoughts down on paper. Sitting there in the choir loft, however, she had no paper. Then she spied the hymn book and, opening to the blank flyleaf, she began jotting the verses of an original poem.

By the time Rev. Schrick finished his sermon, Elvina Hall had completed all four verses of the hymn-poem. After services ended that Sunday, Elvina waited until the parishioners had left and approached her pastor. She handed him the hymnal with her poem written on the flyleaf and explained why she had written it, apologizing for being inattentive during the sermon.

The Rev. Schrick read Mrs. Hall's poem and a strange expression came over his face. He quickly located the paper with Thomas Grape's melody on it and found the words and music matched beautifully!

Three years later, in 1868, Rev. Schrick had the hymn published in a collection entitled *Sabbath Chords*. Since that time, "Jesus Paid It All" has been included in gospel songbooks and hymnals around the world.

How interesting it is that God could move in the heart of an amateur church organist to write a melody for a hymn not yet composed. Then, in his mysterious way, He inspired an unsuspecting choir member to scribble in the flyleaf of her hymnal the words that would perfectly match that melody. And finally, He would lead both the author and composer to give their work to their pastor, who would bring the two together to produce a beautiful musical tribute to God's redemptive work. It is fitting that the chorus reminds the singer of the true author by affirming, "All to Him I owe."

Jesus Paid It All

ELVINA M. HALL

JOHN T. GRAPE

1. I hear the Sav-ior say, "Thy strength in-deed is small,
2. Lord, now in-deed I find Thy pow'r, and thine a - lone,
3. For noth-ing good have I Where - by thy grace to claim;
4. And when, be - fore the throne, I stand in him com - plete,

Child of weak-ness,watch and pray, Find in me thine all in all."
Can change the lep-er's spots And melt the heart of stone.
I'll wash my gar-ments white In the blood of Cal-v'ry's Lamb.
"Je - sus died my soul to save," My lips shall still re - peat.

Je - sus paid it all, All to him I owe;

Sin had left a crim-son stain, He wash'd it white as snow.

A Poet Challenges Convention

・・・・・・・・・・・・・・・・・・・・・・・・・・・・・・・・・・・・・・

Mention great music of the church and complicated oratorios of harmonious choruses or angelic descants might come to mind. How unusual it is, then, that one of the most famous and best loved hymns would consist of only five notes. That, however, is the case with "When I Survey the Wondrous Cross." When Lowell Mason, an important American musician of the nineteenth century, set Isaac Watts' beautiful verses to music, he used an ancient Gregorian chant dating from the sixth century, arranging it into a simple, yet haunting, melody.

But no hymn, however lovely, can stand on music alone, and it is the wedding of words and melody that have made this Communion hymn so popular.

The author, Isaac Watts, was the eldest of nine children born to a well-educated deacon in the Congregational Church of Southampton, England, in 1674. As a child, Watts had an insatiable and inquiring mind. At the age of four he began to study Latin. When he was nine, he took up Greek. By the age of eleven he had added French, and when he was thirteen he decided to conquer Hebrew! He was a poet from the time he could string words together and, as he matured, began to converse in rhyme. His father, frustrated by what he considered an irritating and precocious habit, threatened to spank Isaac if he persisted. Isaac responded with a poetic retort and

Reverend Watts delivered the promised spanking. A tearful, but irrepressible Isaac was said to have vowed, "O father, do some pity take, and I will no more verses make."

Fortunately, for those of us who enjoy great hymns, Isaac Watts did not keep his word. At the age of fifteen, after sitting through a lengthy period of what he considered to be dull and uninspired congregational singing, he complained to his father, "The singing of God's praise is the part of worship nighest heaven, and its performance among us is the worst on earth!" (At that time, the practice was for the leader of the congregation to read a psalm, line by line. The congregation would then repeat each line in a singsong fashion.)

Responding to young Isaac's complaints, his father challenged him to write something better. And so it was that Isaac Watts composed his first hymn. The following week he presented his new hymn to the congregation and it was met with great enthusiasm. Isaac had found a welcome and appreciative audience for his poetry and continued to compose a hymn each week for the next two years. Many of his hymns used favorite psalms in new poetical settings. Two of these still enjoyed today are, "Jesus Shall Reign" and "O God, Our Help in Ages Past."

But the creative mind of Isaac Watts was not content to restate psalms. As he grew older, he ventured into a new area of hymn writing by composing hymns that spoke of personal feelings and emotional responses to the facts and doctrines of the Bible. "When I Survey the Wondrous Cross," written in 1707, was one of the hymns that became very controversial for this reason. It was as if Watts pictured himself at the foot of the cross with Mary and John, gazing in wonder at the crucified Christ. Public criticism of this type of hymn and the stigma of being branded a "radical churchman" didn't seem to bother Watts, nor did it slow his production of beautiful and meaningful hymns. In all, he composed over 600 hymns and earned himself the title of "The Father of English Hymnody."

It was not a title Watts sought, but one suspects he would not have been displeased by it, especially given his response when asked why he devoted himself so tirelessly to the composition of hymns. He said, "It was not my design to exalt myself to the rank and glory of poets; but I was ambitious to be a servant to the churches, and a helper to the joy of the meanest Christian." Isaac Watts achieved his life's goal; the hundreds of Christian hymns he composed have indeed served the churches around the world and brought joy to many a believer.

When I Survey the Wondrous Cross

Isaac Watts

Lowell Mason

1. When I sur-vey the won-drous cross, On which the Prince of glo-ry died, My rich-est gain I count but loss, And pour con-tempt on all my pride.
2. For-bid it, Lord, that I should boast, Save in the death of Christ my God; All the vain things that charm me most, I sac-ri-fice them to his blood.
3. See, from his head, his hands, his feet, Sor-row and love flow min-gled down; Did e'er such love and sor-row meet, Or thorns com-pose so rich a crown.
4. Were the whole realm of na-ture mine, That were a pres-ent far too small; Love so a-maz-ing, so di-vine, De-mands my soul, my life, my all. A-men.

God Rescues a Rebel

In the summer of 1725, in the city of London, England, John Newton was born. His mother, a devout member of the Dissenters, taught the young boy to pray and filled his mind with the Scriptures. But it was John's father, an often-absent sea captain, who captured the boy's imagination. John dreamed of sailing ships and the wide, wild seas, of adventures and mysterious destinations.

Just before John's seventh birthday his mother became ill and died, leaving her son a virtual orphan. Taken in by distant relatives, the little boy was mocked for his belief in God, discouraged from praying, and ridiculed for his childish faith. Unhappy and lonely, John turned again to his dreams of the sea and, at the age of eleven, ran off to become an apprentice on his father's ship.

If it was a close father-son relationship John desired, he was sadly disappointed, for like his foster family, his father also rejected him. For years, the young fellow plied the Mediterranean on sailing ships, enjoying all the experiences and immoralities offered in each exotic port. He was frequently fired for insubordination, but just as frequently hired by another ship's master, eager for young seamen and not too particular about their character.

After a short stint in the British Navy, John deserted and ran away to Africa to seek his fortune and new adventures in the African slave trade. Signing on with an unscrupulous slave dealer, he found his situation had declined dramatically. In the slave trader's absences, John was left in the "care" of the man's vindictive wife, who imprisoned him in her quarters, beat him, and forced him to eat his food from the floor like a dog. Believing death was preferable to this kind of treatment, John escaped from his prison into the West African forests and eventually made his way to the Atlantic Coast. After lighting signal fires, John was finally spotted by a passing ship's captain, who sent a small boat to shore to pick him up.

The captain had hoped the lone man had gold or ivory to offer and was disappointed to receive, instead, a penniless runaway. Putting him to work as a mate, the captain learned later, was an unwise decision. Becoming bored during a particularly long watch, John broke into the ship's supply of rum and generously shared it with the crew. Again demonstrating his lack of discipline, John downed a goodly amount of the liquor, became totally disoriented, and fell overboard. One of the ship's officers, either out of pity or spite, saved John from drowning by spearing him in the thigh with a harpoon and reeling him back aboard like a flailing fish!

Painfully wounded and severely disciplined, Newton was relegated below decks where it was thought he could be no more trouble. It was a miserable journey from Africa to England in the stifling, stinking hold, and John had endless days and nights to ponder his empty life and unfulfilled dreams. Somehow, a copy of Thomas a Kempis' book *Imitation of Christ* fell into his hands. Reading the book awakened his conscience to the things of God, and he began to recall some of the early lessons learned at his mother's knee.

As the slave ship neared Scotland, severe winds and rains battered her and she began to take on water. Desperate measures were taken to keep her from sinking and for days every able-bodied man, slave or free, bailed water from the foundering ship. Exhausted, frightened, and facing certain death, John Newton had a life-transforming experience with God. The assurance of God's love flooded his soul. Later he would describe it as a miracle, an amazing manifestation of God's grace.

Although that voyage was not his last, John Newton's heart became drawn in other directions. Two years after his miraculous conversion, he married Mary Catlett, a devout Christian, and not long after that, John left the sea for good and became a minister. While he loved to preach and tended his little flock of believers with zealous care, his great joy was writing hymns to be sung at his weekly prayer meetings. He composed over 280 hymns, but the one for which he is most remembered came from his shipboard conversion and carries the message of his personal experience, "Amazing Grace."

Amazing Grace

ARR. BY EDWIN O. EXCELL
AMERICAN TRADITIONAL

JOHN NEWTON

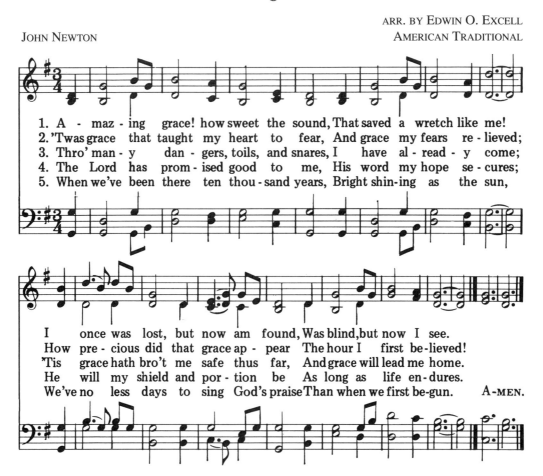

1. A - maz - ing grace! how sweet the sound, That saved a wretch like me!
2. 'Twas grace that taught my heart to fear, And grace my fears re - lieved;
3. Thro' man - y dan - gers, toils, and snares, I have al - read - y come;
4. The Lord has prom - ised good to me, His word my hope se - cures;
5. When we've been there ten thou - sand years, Bright shin - ing as the sun,

I once was lost, but now am found, Was blind, but now I see.
How pre - cious did that grace ap - pear The hour I first be - lieved!
'Tis grace hath bro't me safe thus far, And grace will lead me home.
He will my shield and por - tion be As long as life en - dures.
We've no less days to sing God's praise Than when we first be - gun. A-MEN.

An Invalid's Song of Faith

This beautiful hymn, which is used often at the end of evangelical crusades to inspire men and women to make a commitment to Christ, was actually written by a woman as she languished in the depths of despair. Charlotte Elliott, at the age of forty-five, felt she was useless as a laborer for God. As she lay in her sickbed, she mentally enumerated the things for which she could give thanks and ended up writing them in the verses we now know as "Just As I Am."

Charlotte Elliott lived a carefree and happy life as she grew up in England at the end of the eighteenth century. She was a gifted artist and became popular for her portrait work. In addition to her artistic talents, she wrote humorous verses which were published to some acclaim. With the coming of her thirtieth year, however, Charlotte's health began to fail, and by the time she was thirty-one, she was bedridden. This swift decline in her health and in the ability to enjoy the life she had always known led her to become despondent. As she languished in her bed, month after month, her family became more and more concerned, not only about her physical condition, but about her emotional health as well.

In 1822, the noted Swiss evangelist Henri Cesar Malan was visiting the city of Brighton, England. Charlotte's father invited Dr. Malan to visit their home and asked him to speak with Charlotte. In the course of their conversation, Charlotte told the evangelist that she did not know how to find Christ. Malan's reply was, "Come to Him just as you are."

With that simple encouragement, Charlotte saw the dawn of hope through her depression and made a personal commitment to follow Christ. Her physical health did not change, but her emotional state improved dramatically. From that day on she celebrated what she called a "spiritual birthday" each year to commemorate the day on which she turned over her life to Christ.

Several years passed and Charlotte Elliott's brother, a pastor in a small Brighton parish, was trying to raise enough money to build a school for the children of poor clergymen. To assist in the fund raising, he had organized a bazaar. Members of the parish were hard at work making handicrafts and baked goods to donate. But Charlotte, at home in bed, was frustrated and ill, unable to help, yet longing to do something for the worthwhile cause.

On the day of the bazaar, after the family had left the house, Charlotte was alone in her bed, pondering her situation. She gathered pen and paper and decided to write down the reasons for her trust in Christ. Under the title, "Him that Cometh to Me I Will in No Wise Cast Out, (John 6:37)" she wrote the stanzas we know today as "Just As I Am." It would seem that Dr. Malan's words had come back to comfort her as she repeated them at the beginning of each stanza.

Charlotte's sister-in-law, returning from

the bazaar, found the poem and, without Charlotte's knowledge, had it printed as a leaflet in 1835. The following year it was included in a book of Charlotte's poetry titled *The Invalid's Hymn Book*.

It is interesting to note that although Charlotte had despaired over her inability to help out her brother's building project, it was her hymn, "Just As I Am" that brought in more funds than all the other money-raising projects combined! In a letter, her brother wrote, "In the course of a long ministry, I hope to have been permitted to see some fruit of my labors; but I feel more has been done by a single hymn of my sister's."

While she was plagued with illness, pain, and fatigue for over fifty-one years, Charlotte Elliott wrote several books and over 150 hymns, many of which were especially aimed at comforting those who were ill or suffering. When she died on September 22, 1871, at the age of eighty-two, she left a rich legacy. In the years since she wrote "Just As I Am," countless Christians have shared her experience of faith and renewed their commitment to Christ through her simple, yet moving words.

Just As I Am

Charlotte Elliot

Phillip Landgrave

1. Just as I am, with-out one plea, But that thy
2. Just as I am, and wait-ing not To rid my
3. Just as I am, tho tossed a-bout With man-y a
4. Just as I am, poor, wretch-ed, blind; Sight, rich - es,
5. Just as I am, thou wilt re-ceive, Wilt wel - come,
6. Just as I am, thy love un-known Hath bro - ken

blood was shed for me, And that thou bidd'st me
soul of one dark blot, To thee whose blood can
con - flict, many a doubt, Fight-ings with - in and
heal - ing of the mind, Yea, all I need in
par - don, cleanse, re - lieve, Be - cause thy prom - ise
ev - 'ry bar - rier down; Now to be thine, yea,

come to thee, O Lamb of God, I come! I come!
cleanse each spot, O Lamb of God, I come! I come!
fears with - out, O Lamb of God, I come! I come!
thee to find, O Lamb of God, I come! I come!
I be - lieve, O Lamb of God, I come! I come!
thine a - lone, O Lamb of God, I come! I come!

Convicted by the Cross

• •

Hymn pollsters report that "The Old Rugged Cross" is the most frequently requested hymn; and songbook editors have designated it as the most popular of all twentieth-century religious songs. Within thirty years of its initial publication in 1913, more than twenty million copies of "The Old Rugged Cross" had been sold, outselling every other musical composition of any kind published to that date! What is it that makes this gospel song so popular?

It has been speculated that the author and composer of this hymn, George Bennard, was a clever hymn writer who knew the tricks of wedding a swinging melody, a good chorus, and easily memorized words. Others who have tried to evaluate the reasons for the hymn's popularity say it grabs the heart of the singer with raw emotionalism. Still others claim its success lies in the presentation of the truth of the Gospel story in terms every believer can appreciate, bringing firm reality to the theological doctrines regarding the cross of Christ. For the author, however, the hymn was not written to become a great success, but in answer to a deep personal need in his own life. And perhaps that is the reason it has meant so much through the years to others, as they feel it meets a deep need in their lives, too.

Born in Youngstown, Ohio, on February 4, 1873, George Bennard was raised in a loving family, the only son among four daughters. While he was still quite young, the family moved to Lucas, Iowa. It was here, while attending a revival meeting sponsored by the Salvation Army, that Bennard made a personal commitment to follow Christ.

When George was only sixteen years old, his father died, and he assumed the responsibility of providing for his mother and four sisters. When his family responsibilities lessened, Bennard joined the Salvation Army, where he initially served alone and then, after his marriage, with his wife. Both Bennard and his wife were officers with the Salvation Army until he felt the call to move on into a different area of ministry. Resigning his position with the Salvation Army, he became a traveling evangelist for the Methodist church. As such he conducted revival campaigns in Canada and in the northern and central United States.

One time, after an especially difficult experience in a New York campaign, Bennard returned to his home in Michigan. There he reflected on the meaning of the cross in the life of a believer, especially in light of the Bible passage from Galatians 6:14 in which the Apostle Paul states: "May I never boast except in the cross of our Lord Jesus Christ, through which the world has been crucified to me, and I to the world."

Considering these words, Bennard became convinced that the cross was not merely a symbol of Christianity, but the very heart of it. In his writings, Bennard reports that as he meditated upon this, the words, "the old rugged cross," came into his mind and then the notes of a melody ran through his head. Quickly, he wrote them down and then tried for several weeks to compose words to fit the tune. Finally, after a period of prayer, the poetry of the verses began to flow from his pen almost unbidden. After completing the four verses of the hymn and the chorus, Bennard took the hymn to the home of some friends, the Reverend and Mrs. L.O. Bostwick, and sang it for them. He concluded his presentation with the question, "Will it do?" The Bostwicks were so enthusiastic about the hymn that they offered to pay the fees to have it printed. Consequently, "The Old Rugged Cross" was published for the first time in 1915, and has been met with enthusiasm from that day to this.

After writing this hymn, George Bennard went on to travel and preach for another forty years. Although he composed several other hymns, none was to become as popular as his first. In 1958, at the age of eighty-five, he "exchanged his cross for a crown." George Bennard was honored in his hometown of Reed City, Michigan. Near the house where he died, the city officials erected a wooden cross that stands twelve feet high. On it is a plaque that reads:"'The Old Rugged Cross'—Home of George Bennard, composer of the beloved hymn."

The Old Rugged Cross

GEORGE BENNARD

GEORGE BENNARD

1. On a hill far a - way stood an old rug-ged cross, The em-blem of
2. Oh, that old rug-ged cross so de-spised by the world, Has a won-drous at-
3. In the old rug-ged cross, stained with blood so divine, A won - drous
4. To the old rug-ged cross I will ev - er be true, Its shame and re-

suf - f'ring and shame; And I love that old cross where the dear - est and best
trac - tion for me; For the dear Lamb of God left his glo - ry a - bove,
beau - ty I see; For 'twas on that old cross Je - sus suf - fered and died,
proach glad-ly bear; Then he'll call me some day to my home far a - way,

For a world of lost sin - ners was slain.
To bear it to dark Cal - va - ry. So I'll cher - ish the old rug-ged
To par - don and sanc - ti - fy me. cross, the
Where his glo - ry for - ev - er I'll share.

cross, Till my tro-phies at last I lay down; I will cling to the
old rug-ged cross,

old rug-ged cross, And ex-change it some day for a crown.
cross, the old rug-ged cross,

HYMNS OF HOPE

Friendship's Inspiration

It was a hot day in Elkhorn, Wisconsin, and Sanford Fillmore Bennett sat in his stuffy office reviewing some paperwork. At that moment a friend, Joseph Webster, knocked on the door. Calling for him to enter, Bennett looked up to see his friend come into the office looking downcast. As Webster slumped into a chair, his friend asked him what the trouble was. Webster shook his head, sighed, and replied, "Oh it will be all right by and by."

The two men then began to chat, but the phrase—"by and by"—kept repeating itself in Bennett's mind. Finally, as their conversation came to a close, Bennett commented, "You know, what you said earlier would make a great line for a gospel song. 'By and by; by and by'—how about 'the sweet by and by?'"

Webster, roused out of his melancholy by the conversation and the suggestion of composing a song using his words, began to hum a tune. Bennett grabbed a piece of paper and a pen and jotted down the first verse: "There's a land that is fairer than day, and by faith we can see it afar, for the Father waits over the way, to prepare us a dwelling place

there." Webster left the office for a few minutes and returned with a friend who carried a violin. Together the three men composed both the words and melody to this famous gospel song, well known for its chorus: "In the sweet by and by, we shall meet on the beautiful shore."

This hymn was one of the many gospel choruses composed in the United States during the mid-nineteenth century. It became popular as it was sung at traveling camp meetings and singing schools throughout the midwestern and eastern states. In the latter years of the nineteenth century, "In the Sweet By and By" became a favorite of the members of the Salvation Army and is still often sung at Army funeral services.

This simple gospel song of hope wasn't the product of a great religious debate or an outpouring of grief or gratitude; it was just the spontaneous result of a short conversation between two friends. But it speaks to the hearts of humble believers everywhere who look forward to their heavenly home with faith and assurance that it will be a place of joy and peace where loved ones will once more be united.

In the Sweet By and By

Sanford F. Bennet

Joseph P. Webster

Verses from a Vision

・・・・・・・・・・・・・・・・・・・・・・・・・・・・・・・・・・・・・

Favorite hymns have been written by evangelists and preachers, great pillars of the church, and revolutionaries, but this is probably the only well-known hymn written by a pharmacist! C. Austin Miles was born in New Jersey in January of 1868. He attended the Philadelphia College of Pharmacy and graduated from the University of Pennsylvania. He then obtained a position as a pharmacist and worked in that field for several years. During that time, he wrote his first gospel song. When it received a degree of popularity, Miles decided gospel music was more rewarding than pharmacy and left his profession for a career in publishing. In 1898, at the age of thirty, he took a full-time position with the Hall-Mack Publishing Company in Philadelphia, where he was to serve as editor and manager for the next four decades.

It was during this period that music publisher Dr. Adam Geibel approached Miles with the suggestion that he write a hymn text that would be "sympathetic in tone, breathing tenderness in every line; one that would bring hope to the hopeless, rest for the weary, and downy pillows to dying beds."

Shortly after receiving Geibel's suggestion, the unusual circumstances of the writing of "In the Garden" occurred. Miles himself recounts the occasion in George W. Sanville's book, *Forty Gospel Hymn Stories*:

> One day in March, 1912, in the darkroom where I kept my photographic equipment and organ, I drew my Bible toward me; it opened at the favorite chapter, John 20—whether by chance or inspiration let each reader decide. That meeting of Jesus and Mary had lost none of its power to charm. As I read it that day, I seemed to be part of the scene. I became a silent witness to that dramatic moment in Mary's life, when she knelt before her Lord, and cried, '*Rabboni*!' My hands were resting on the Bible while I stared at the light blue wall.

Miles continues to describe how, in a vivid vision, the scene of Mary Magdalene coming to the empty tomb at daybreak was enacted before him on the wall of his darkroom. He recalls witnessing Mary's initial despair and then her joy as she recognizes the gardener as her Lord, the risen Christ. He continues:

> I awakened in full light, gripping the Bible, with muscles tense and nerves vibrating. Under the inspiration of the vision I wrote as quickly as the words could be formed the poem exactly as it has since appeared. That same evening I wrote the music.

The first two verses of the hymn detail the scene through Mary's eyes as she comes to the garden "while the dew is still on the roses," and how she rejoices to recognize the voice as belonging to the Son of God. In the third verse, she relates the command of her Savior to go and tell of her experience.

Some students of religious music have criticized Miles' hymn as being a sentimental song about the joys of a garden at daybreak, but the experience of the author and the close connection with the Scripture passages in John 20 support the fact that it is, indeed, an inspired message of hope and encouragement. Its popularity as a Gospel favorite, second only to "The Old Rugged Cross," speaks well of its ability to touch the lives of those who sing it in churches everywhere.

C. Austin Miles wrote additional religious anthems and cantatas in the years prior to his death in 1946, but he was said to have felt his gospel hymns had made the greatest contribution to the average person. Certainly the thousands who have been blessed by the beautiful verses of "In the Garden" would be among the first to agree.

In the Garden

C. Austin Miles

C. Austin Miles

1. I come to the gar-den a-lone, While the dew is
2. He speaks, and the sound of his voice Is so sweet the
3. I'd stay in the gar-den with him Tho the night a-

still on the ros-es; And the voice I hear, fall-ing on my ear,
birds hush their sing-ing; And the mel-o-dy that he gave to me
round me be fall-ing; But he bids me go; thro' the voice of woe,

The Son of God dis-clos-es.
With-in my heart is ring-ing. And he walks with me, and he
His voice to me is call-ing.

talks with me, And he tells me I am his own, And the joy we

share as we tar-ry there, None oth-er has ev-er known.

The Triumph of Faith over Sight

. . . .

If anyone ever had cause to be discouraged and depressed it was Fanny Crosby. As an infant she was accidentally blinded by a country doctor's application of a mustard poultice to her eyes. Her father passed away while she was a small child. She married at the age of thirty-eight and her only child died in infancy. After twenty-five years of marriage, she was widowed and lived the remainder of her life, thirty-two additional years, alone. Yet this tiny and energetic woman never became bitter or morose. Her spirit was one of joy and enthusiasm and a little poem she wrote at the age of eight seemed to be the theme of her long and fruitful life:

Oh, what a happy soul am I,
Although I cannot see,
I am resolved that in this world
Contented I will be.
How many blessings I enjoy
That other people don't!
To weep and sigh because I'm blind,
I cannot, and I won't!

Fanny Crosby's resolution to enjoy life and to be appreciative of her many blessings was translated into a full and active life, one that would contribute to the religious heritage of the United States in a remarkable and lasting way.

As is immediately obvious from the lovely poem above, Fanny possessed a gift for rhyming at an early age. She also had an acute memory and great gifts of insight and deep concentration. At the age of fifteen, she was sent to the New York Institute for the Blind, where she learned to read Braille and eventually, to teach. After completing her education at the Institute, she served as a member of its faculty for eleven years. During the latter years of her teaching assignment, she met and married Alexander van Alstyne, a blind musician.

After leaving the teaching profession, Fanny devoted much of her time to writing popular songs that were set to music by G. F. Root. In 1864, Fanny was introduced to William Bradbury, a pioneer in writing music for American Sunday schools. Bradbury was impressed by Fanny's poetic gifts, and he challenged her to turn her talents to writing Christian songs and hymns. From that time forth, it is reported that she never wrote another secular song, concentrating all her talents and energies on composing verses for gospel singing.

She wrote under her own name as well as under over 200 pseudonyms. Her lifetime production of hymns has been estimated to exceed 8,000! It is said that she prayed fervently prior to setting pen to paper and that many of her hymns seemed to flow from her mind as fluidly as her conversation. Such it was with the composition of "Blessed Assurance."

One afternoon in 1873, Fanny was visiting with her good friend Mrs. Joseph Knapp, the wife of the founder of the Metropolitan

Life Insurance Company. Mrs. Knapp was an amateur musician who enjoyed composing melodies. On this occasion, she had a new one she wanted to play for her friend. She played the tune through once and asked Fanny, "What does this tune say?" Fanny knelt there in the Knapp's parlor and Mrs. Knapp played the melody over again. Suddenly, Fanny smiled and rose to her feet announcing: "It says, 'Blessed Assurance, Jesus is mine, Oh what a foretaste of glory divine!'" Fanny continued to dictate the verses and Mrs. Knapp wrote them down, joining them to her melody as we have them today.

This was just one of the thousands of hymns Fanny Crosby wrote in her full and fruitful life. Others that might be familiar are: "Tell Me the Story of Jesus," "Praise Him! Praise Him!" "Draw Me Nearer," "Near the Cross," "Take the World, but Give Me Jesus," "To God Be the Glory," "Rescue the Perishing," "He Hideth My Soul," and "Pass Me Not, O Gentle Savior."

When Fanny Crosby died, six weeks before her ninety-fifth birthday, she left the world a rich legacy of gospel songs. Throughout the past century, millions of Christians all over the world have been inspired and encouraged by her words. Yet on her tombstone, at Bridgeport, Connecticut, there is a simple inscription that sums up her attitude of humility. It is a portion of Scripture taken from the remarks of Jesus when he was questioned about the woman at Bethany who had anointed his head with costly perfume. It reads: "She hath done what she could."

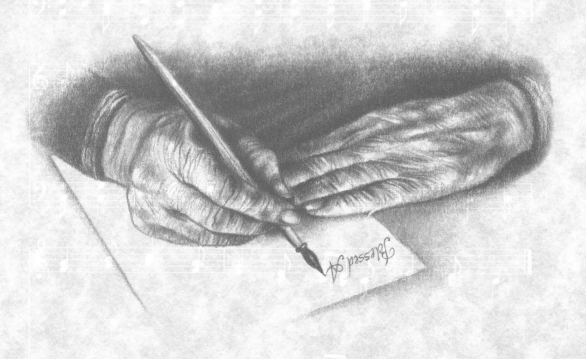

Blessed Assurance

FANNY J. CROSBY

PHOEBE P. KNAPP

1. Bless-ed as-sur-ance, Je-sus is mine! Oh, what a fore-taste of
2. Per-fect sub-mis-sion, per-fect de-light, Vi-sions of rap-ture now
3. Per-fect sub-mis-sion, all is at rest, I in my Sav-ior am

glo-ry di-vine! Heir of sal-va-tion, pur-chase of God,
burst on my sight: An-gels de-scend-ing bring from a-bove
hap-py and blest: Watch-ing and wait-ing, look-ing a-bove,

Born of his Spir-it, wash'd in his blood.
Ech-oes of mer-cy, whis-pers of love. This is my sto-ry, this is my
Fill'd with his good-ness, lost in his love.

song, Prais-ing my Sav-ior all the day long; This is my sto-ry,

this is my song, Prais-ing my Sav-ior all the day long.

A Son's Challenge—A Mother's Faith

I n the field of Christian ministry there have been many husband and wife teams that have worked together to spread the Gospel. Civilla Martin and her husband, Stillman, were just such a couple.

Civilla was born on August 21, 1869, in Nova Scotia. She was educated there and then went on to study music and teach school before her marriage to Stillman. At the time of their marriage, Stillman was an ordained Baptist minister, having received his college education at Harvard University. Dr. and Mrs. Martin traveled throughout the United States, holding evangelistic meetings and Bible conferences. Mrs. Martin assisted her husband with the teaching and also contributed hymn texts appropriate to the subjects of his sermons on occasion.

In 1904 the Martins and their young son were spending several weeks in Lestershire, New York, at the Practical Bible Training School. Dr. Martin was collaborating with the president of the school, John Davis, in the preparation of a gospel songbook for use in Bible meetings.

During the stay in Lestershire, Civilla became very ill and was confined to her bed. Stillman had a preaching engagement one evening when she seemed especially weak and was considering cancelling it because of her condition. As they discussed the situation, their young son quietly entered the room and stood listening. Suddenly he piped up, "Father, don't you think that if God wants you to preach today, He will take care of Mother while you are away?" The boy's words of assurance and childlike faith gave Dr. Martin the encouragement he needed to keep his preaching commitment.

Faithful to his congregation, Stillman kept his appointment to preach, and several in the crowd were so moved by his message from the Bible that they made professions of faith in Christ at the close of his sermon. Feeling that God had certainly blessed his preaching, Dr. Martin hurried home to share the good news with his wife and son.

When he entered the house where they were staying, he found that his wife had not only improved remarkably, but she had also had the energy and inspiration to write a hymn text based on the words their son had spoken to them earlier in the day. She had entitled the text, "God Will Take Care of You" and handed it to her husband with a smile as he asked how she was feeling.

There was a small portable organ in the house and Stillman took the sheet with the verses on it, placed it on the instrument and began composing a melody to accompany his wife's text. Before long, he had written a lovely melody. He gathered a couple of other teachers from the school; together they sang the new hymn that very evening. They were all so enthusiastic about the encouraging message of the words and the blending of text and melody that they performed the hymn at the Bible Training School later in the week. The students and teachers were equally as impressed with the Martins' hymn and John

Davis suggested they include it in the songbook they were compiling. Thus it was that "God Will Take Care of You" was published in 1905 in *Songs of Redemption and Praise*. From that time to the present, this hymn of comfort has been a favorite of Christians everywhere.

Hymns of Hope

God Will Take Care of You

CIVILLA D. MARTIN

W. STILLMAN MARTIN

1. Be not dis-may'd what-e'er be-tide, God will take care of you;
2. Thro' days of toil when heart doth fail, God will take care of you;
3. No mat-ter what may be the test, God will take care of you;

Be-neath his wings of love a-bide, God will take care of you.
When dan-gers fierce your path as-sail, God will take care of you.
Lean, wea-ry one, up-on his breast, God will take care of you.

God will take care of you, Thro' ev-'ry day, o'er all the way;

He will take care of you, God will take care of you.

Answering the Call

Music was always an important part of James Milton Black's life, and from an early age he demonstrated not only an avid interest, but also an aptitude for composing, playing, and singing. Born at South Hill, New York, on August 19, 1856, young James was educated in the arts of singing and playing the organ. After completing his formal education, Black became a teacher of singing schools. He traveled around the countryside, stopping in small towns and villages where he would enroll local students for a week or two in his singing courses. As the lessons progressed, Black introduced his students to the rudiments of musical interpretation, including sight reading, conducting, and choral singing. At the end of the course, a recital would be held and the students would demonstrate their musical abilities before the entire community.

In addition to his successful singing schools, James Black worked as an editor of gospel songbooks. The books he edited were then published by either the Methodist Book Concerns or the Hall-Mack Company in Philadelphia. One of his collections, *Songs of the Soul*, published in 1894, was extremely popular, selling over 400,000 copies in its first two years of publication.

Although not a member of the clergy, James Black took an active part in the life of his home church, the Williamsport, Pennsylvania, Methodist Church. There he taught Sunday school and was the president of the Young People's Society. He found great joy in ministering to the youth in the community and often spent much time and energy encouraging young persons who had unhappy or difficult home situations. Thus it was that Black became a friend and counselor to a fourteen-year-old girl who had the misfortune to be the daughter of the town drunkard. He encouraged her to attend Sunday school and to join the Young People's Society where she soon became a regular attendee and faithful believer.

Black encouraged his young students to memorize Scripture verses and frequently required them to recite a favorite verse from the Bible in answer to the roll call at the weekly youth meetings. One week, when the name of the young girl in whom he had taken a special interest was called, there was no response. Her absence sparked a spiritual application in Black's mind and he took advantage of the situation to make reference to a passage from chapter twenty of the Book of Revelation, which speaks of the Lamb's Book of Life. He told his students what a sad thing it would be, when the names are called from that heavenly book, if anyone were absent. Concluding his remarks, he cried, "O God, when my own name is called up yonder, may I be there to respond!"

As he walked home that evening after the church meeting, James Black could not rid his mind of those words and wished he had known a song he might have used to impress his young congregation with the importance of being at that heavenly roll-call. The words

"Why don't you make it?" seemed to echo in his mind.

Black was completely preoccupied with thoughts of such a song as he entered his home. When his wife commented on his troubled expression, he made no reply. The verses were already beginning to take form. Black went to his desk, set pen to paper and, within fifteen minutes, had written all three verses of the song. Taking the stanzas to the piano, he reports that he sat down, put his fingers on the keys, and played the music out from beginning to end. Later in his life he was quoted as saying, "I have never dared to change a single word or a note of the piece since."

As a poignant postscript to the story, Black was saddened to learn that his young friend was absent from the meeting because of illness, diagnosed a few days later as pneumonia. Within two weeks, she had died, unable to ever answer another roll-call here on earth, but most certainly she was present when her name was called "up yonder."

Hymns of Hope

When the Roll Is Called up Yonder

JAMES M. BLACK

JAMES M. BLACK

1. When the trum-pet of the Lord shall sound, and time shall be no more,
2. On that bright and cloudless morning when the dead in Christ shall rise,
3. Let us la - bor for the Mas-ter from the dawn till set-ting sun,

And the morn-ing breaks, e - ter - nal, bright, and fair; When the
And the glo - ry of his res - ur - rec - tion share; When his
Let us talk of all his won-drous love and care; Then when

saved of earth shall gath - er o - ver on the oth - er shore,
cho - sen ones shall gath - er to their home be - yond the skies,
all of life is o - ver, and our work on earth is done,

And the roll is called up yon - der, I'll be there. When the

roll is called up yon - der, When the
When the roll is called up yon - der, I'll be there,

roll is called up yon - der, When the roll is
When the roll is called up yon-der, I'll be there, When the roll is

called up yon - der, When the roll is called up yon - der, I'll be there.

HYMNS OF PEACE

The Carver and the Composer

The information we have about the author of this favorite gospel hymn has come not from the author himself, but from a friend to whom the poem was dictated. In 1842, in the town of Coleshill, Warwickshire, England, the Rev. Thomas Salmon stopped by a small trinket shop to visit with his friend, William Walford. Walford was seventy years old at the time and his eyesight was almost gone. Nevertheless, he ran the tiny shop where he sold small carvings and engraved items.

On this particular day, Walford asked his friend to copy down the verses to a prayer-poem he had been composing in his head. Salmon took pen and paper and wrote the words to the gospel hymn we now call "Sweet Hour of Prayer." Thomas Salmon was so impressed with Walford's poem that he made a second copy of it for himself and tucked this away in his notes and papers.

Three years later, Salmon traveled to the United States; while in New York City, he sent Walford's poem to the editor of the *New York Observer*. The editor was so impressed with the prayer-poem that he published it in the September 13, 1845, issue of his paper. In addition to the text of the poem, the paper carried Salmon's tale of having received it by dictation from his blind friend, a carver of trinkets back home in England.

The possibility of the poem becoming a hymn was appreciated by the compilers of a Baptist Hymnal in 1859, and they included it in a book entitled *Church Melodies* published that same year.

Still, it wasn't until William Bradbury, noted American composer of gospel music, set the words to music in 1861 and then published the words and music together in his collection of hymns, *The Golden Chain,* that the general public began to appreciate and enjoy the comforting message of this hymn.

William Bradbury was well-known in the mid-1800s for taking a simple religious poem and giving it wings with his music. Although he was a gifted musician and composer and could have gained fame and prosperity in the field of secular music, Bradbury's heart was drawn to writing quality melodies for songs to be sung in Sunday schools. He disagreed with the trend in those days of using popular secular tunes as accompaniments for religious hymns. In his efforts to change this trend, he became known as the "pioneer of Sunday school songs." In all, he published sixty songbooks containing the melodies for the following favorites, as well as many others: "Jesus Loves Me," "Just As I Am," "My Hope Is Built on Nothing Else," "He Leadeth Me," and "Savior Like a Shepherd Lead Us."

"Sweet Hour of Prayer" was the result of international co-operation: a blind poet and his pastor friend in England who shared their work with a newspaper editor and a composer in New York. The result was a hymn that has strengthened and encouraged faith on both sides of the Atlantic for over 140 years, proving once more that the power of prayer is not limited by political or geographical boundaries.

Sweet Hour of Prayer

William Walford   William B. Bradbury

1. Sweet hour of prayer, sweet hour of prayer, That calls me from a world of care And bids me at my Father's throne Make all my wants and wish-es known! In sea-sons of dis-tress and grief, My soul has oft-en found re-lief, And oft es-caped the tempt-er's snare By thy re-turn, sweet hour of prayer.

2. Sweet hour of prayer, sweet hour of prayer, Thy wings shall my pe-ti-tion bear To him whose truth and faith-ful-ness En-gage the wait-ing soul to bless: And since he bids me seek his face, Be-lieve his word and trust his grace, I'll cast on him my ev-'ry care, And wait for thee, sweet hour of prayer.

3. Sweet hour of prayer, sweet hour of prayer, May I thy con-so-la-tion share, Till, from *Mount Pisgah's loft-y height, I view my home and take my flight: This robe of flesh I'll drop and rise To seize the ev-er-last-ing prize; And shout, while pass-ing thro' the air, "Fare-well, fare-well, sweet hour of prayer!"

Strength out of Weakness

I t is an ironic truth that many of the greatest saints endure life in the weakest bodies. Such was the case with Henry F. Lyte, a pillar of the Church of England who battled poor health all his life. Perhaps it was this close acquaintance with earthly weakness that provided him with the ability to see so clearly the strength of God, and to convey it so powerfully in his poetry, music, and sermons.

From his childhood, Lyte suffered with asthma, yet he persevered with his Biblical studies and earned a Doctorate from Trinity College in Dublin, Ireland. After graduation, he took a succession of small parishes, finally settling in the fishing village of Lower Brixham, Devonshire, England, in 1824, at the age of thirty-one.

The sturdy fishermen and burly soldiers from a nearby garrison who comprised Lyte's congregation made a striking contrast with their frail and sickly pastor. Lyte, however, provided constant encouragement and spiritual food to his flock and was well-loved for his caring ways and kindly words.

Dr. Lyte frequently ignored his own infirmities and ailments to preach and visit the sick and was reported to have coined the maxim: "It is better to wear out than to rust out." His words seemed prophetic when, in the late 1840s, his physician gave him the news that he suffered from tuberculosis and didn't have long to live. Not willing to give in to the disease that plagued him, Henry Lyte continued, as always, his pastoral responsibilities. By the summer of 1847, however, it became clear that even if his spirit was willing, his body would not be able to maintain the pace. Reluctantly taking his doctor's advice, Lyte made plans to move to the warmer climate of Rome, Italy, and to enjoy the recuperative powers of the sunny Italian countryside. On his last Sunday in Brixham, he practically had to crawl into the pulpit to deliver his sermon. Perhaps because of a renewed sense of his own mortality, he spoke passionately on the need for his parishioners to prepare for the time when they would have to face their Maker. Leaving the pulpit, Lyte returned to his study, where he penned the beautiful and comforting hymn, "Abide with Me." That evening he handed the hymn to a relative and prepared for his journey to Italy.

Following the trip across the English Channel and a carriage ride through the French countryside, Lyte reached Nice, France. He was so weak after his journey that he could not continue and took to his bed. A few weeks later, on November 20, 1847, Henry Lyte died. He was buried at the English cemetery at Nice.

After his death, Lyte's hymn, "Abide with Me," seemed to take on a life of its own. It was translated into dozens of languages, and the deeply personal nature of the lyrics became meaningful to believers of all nationalities and ages. When the centenary of Lyte's death was remembered in 1947, letters poured in attesting to the comfort and assurance his hymn had provided in times of deep despair and even death.

A group of ex-prisoners of war from England recalled how they sang the hymn each Sunday evening while imprisoned. Survivors of the *Titanic* catastrophe told of hearing the strains of "Abide with Me" sung by the doomed passengers standing on the sinking ship as it slipped beneath the sea. Belgian survivors of Word War I reported that the words of "Abide with Me" were on the lips of British nurse Edith Cavel as she faced a German firing squad in 1915, condemned for her part in sheltering British, French, and Belgian soldiers.

Perhaps the most appropriate explanation for the hymn's great popularity was penned by an anonymous English woman who sent the following tribute to the *London Sunday Times*:

Its secret is its great simplicity: it is easily grasped and understood by the ordinary man and its greatness, depth, and beauty must appeal to scholars and thoughtful men whatever their religious conviction or creed.

Abide with Me

Henry F. Lyte

William H. Monk

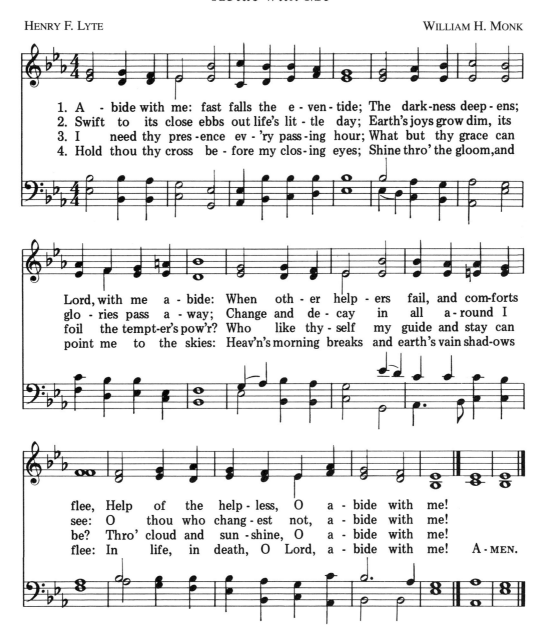

1. A - bide with me: fast falls the e - ven - tide; The dark-ness deep-ens;
2. Swift to its close ebbs out life's lit - tle day; Earth's joys grow dim, its
3. I need thy pres-ence ev - 'ry pass-ing hour; What but thy grace can
4. Hold thou thy cross be - fore my clos-ing eyes; Shine thro' the gloom, and

Lord, with me a - bide: When oth - er help - ers fail, and com-forts
glo - ries pass a - way; Change and de - cay in all a - round I
foil the tempt-er's pow'r? Who like thy - self my guide and stay can
point me to the skies: Heav'n's morning breaks and earth's vain shad-ows

flee, Help of the help - less, O a - bide with me!
see: O thou who chang - est not, a - bide with me!
be? Thro' cloud and sun - shine, O a - bide with me!
flee: In life, in death, O Lord, a - bide with me! A - MEN.

A Homemaker's Prayer

● ●

The author of this deeply personal hymn of hope was a thirty-seven-year-old mother and homemaker. She held no degree in theology nor any place of great responsibility in her church, yet her simple and heartfelt verses have been a blessing to countless Christians over the past century.

Annie Sherwood Hawks was born on May 28, 1835, in the town of Hoosick, New York. As a child she loved poetry and began writing original verses when she was still in grammar school. By the age of fourteen she was successful in getting her poems published and had become a regular contributor to several newspapers. At the age of twenty-four, Annie married Charles Hawks, and they moved to Brooklyn, New York, where they raised a family of three children. Annie kept busy with the children and the home, and it was while she was thus occupied that the words of her famous prayer-poem, "I Need Thee Every Hour," came to her. She recalls it this way in her writings:

> One day as a young wife and mother of thirty-seven years of age, I was busy with my regular household tasks during a bright June morning, in 1872. Suddenly, I became filled with a sense of nearness to the Master, and I began to wonder how anyone could ever live without Him, either in joy or pain. Then, the words were ushered into my mind and these thoughts took possession of me—'I need Thee every hour.'

As the words flowed into her mind, Annie Hawks seated herself at a desk beside an open window. With the bright June sunshine streaming through the window, and the early summer breezes fluttering the curtains, she wrote the lines of this poem. She had not thought of them as a hymn, but as a poetic prayer. One day, however, she decided to show her composition to her pastor, Dr. Robert Lowry.

Besides being the pastor at the Baptist Church in Brooklyn, Lowry was an accomplished gospel hymn writer and had composed such gospel favorites as: "Shall We Gather at the River" and "Marching to Zion." When Lowry read Annie Hawks' poem, he saw in it the makings of another gospel hymn. Dr. Lowry added the refrain and wrote a simple, but catchy melody.

The hymn was first published that same year in a pamphlet of hymns used at the National Baptist Sunday School Convention held in Cincinnati, Ohio. After that occasion, when it was well-received by the delegates to the convention, the hymn was printed in a new song book by Lowry and William Doane entitled *The Royal Diadem*. A few years later, when Ira Sankey and Dwight Moody held their huge evangelistic campaigns across the United States and in Great Britain, "I Need Thee Every Hour" became a popular favorite on both sides of the Atlantic.

Although appreciative of the hymn's popularity, Annie Hawks could never put her finger on a reason for the song's ability to touch so many in such a meaningful way until a personal grief brought the comforting message of her hymn home to her. In 1888, Charles Hawks died, and his widow Annie described the time of sorrow following his death as a "shadow of great loss" cast over her life. In this dark hour her own hymn ministered to her and she wrote: "I understood something of the comforting power in the words, which I had been permitted to give out to others in my hour of sweet serenity and peace."

"I Need Thee Every Hour" was a simple poem written by a simple homemaker from a heart of simple faith, but it has brought a message of deep meaning to men and women from all walks of life for over 125 years.

I Need Thee Every Hour

ANNIE S. HAWKS

ROBERT LOWRY

1. I need thee ev - 'ry hour, Most gra - cious Lord;
2. I need thee ev - 'ry hour, Stay thou near by;
3. I need thee ev - 'ry hour, In joy or pain;
4. I need thee ev - 'ry hour, Teach me thy will;
5. I need thee ev - 'ry hour, Most Ho - ly One;

No ten - der voice like thine Can peace af - ford.
Temp - ta - tions lose their pow'r When thou art nigh.
Come quick - ly and a - bide, Or life is vain.
Thy prom - is - es so rich In me ful - fill.
O make me thine in - deed, Thou bless - ed Son.

I need thee, O I need thee; Ev - 'ry hour I need thee!

O bless me now, my Sav - ior, I come to thee. A - MEN.

A Friend to the Friendless

· ·

This favorite hymn about the unfailing friendship of Jesus was written by a man who had few close friends on earth. He had experienced the sorrows of grief and loneliness; and he had poured out his life in service to others without thought to repayment of any kind. In fact, it was said of Joseph Scriven that he would only work for those who could not pay!

Born into a prosperous Irish family on September 10, 1819, Joseph Scriven successfully completed the requirements for entrance to Trinity College in Dublin, but after attending for only a short time, he decided to leave and join the army. His military career, however, was cut short by poor health and he returned to Trinity College, where he earned his Bachelor of Arts Degree.

With his education behind him and a long and happy life ahead, Joseph Scriven decided to wed his sweetheart. But the night before their wedding, tragedy struck. Scriven's fiancee was thrown from the horse she was riding and into a river, where she was drowned. Overcome with grief, Scriven became despondent and introspective and withdrew from his friends and family. He made the decision to leave the religious traditions of his parents in favor of those of the Plymouth Brethren. In connection with that decision, he determined to leave his homeland and migrate to Canada in 1844, at the age of twenty-five.

With the move, Scriven refocused his life to concentrate on living the lifestyle described by Christ in the Sermon on the Mount. He became a servant of the underprivileged, assisting the handicapped, the poverty-stricken, the ill, and the imprisoned. He cut and hauled wood for destitute families so they might survive the frigid winters of Port Hope, Ontario. Although he was respected by the townspeople for his deeds of mercy, he was viewed as an eccentric and was not integrated into their fellowship. Nonetheless, Scriven met and fell in love with a young Canadian woman and again planned to marry. But before the wedding took place, once more tragedy struck as the young woman contracted pneumonia and died.

At the same time, Scriven received news that his mother, back in Dublin, was seriously ill. He did not have the funds to finance a trip home, so he wrote the three verses of a poem he titled "Pray without Ceasing," and sent them to his mother hoping they would lift her spirits and comfort her.

Some time later, when Scriven himself was confined to his bed with illness, a neighbor stopped in to see him. As they talked, the friend saw a paper at the side of the bed with the words of Scriven's poem scrawled on it. After reading the poem, the man inquired if Scriven had written it. He replied, "The Lord and I did it between us." Securing Scriven's permission, the neighbor saw to it that the poem was published in a small collection of poetry called *Hymns and Other Verses*.

Some time later, Charles Converse, a well-known composer of that day, wrote a melody for the verses Scriven had penned. The hymn was then retitled "What a Friend We Have in Jesus" after the first line of the text.

On a cold morning in October of 1886, the body of Joseph Scriven was found in Rice Lake in Bawdly, Ontario. He had departed from his lonely life and gone to be with his best friend Jesus. And in his memory the citizens of Port Hope, Ontario, erected a simple monument. On its face they inscribed the words of Scriven's hymn. The last line reflects the author's final hope: "In His arms He'll take and shield thee. Thou wilt find a solace there."

I AM THE GOOD SHEPHERD. JOHN 10:11

What a Friend We Have in Jesus

JOSEPH SCRIVEN

CHARLES C. CONVERSE

1. What a friend we have in Je-sus, All our sins and griefs to bear!
2. Have we tri-als and temp-ta-tions? Is there trou-ble an-y-where?
3. Are we weak and heav-y lad-en, Cum-bered with a load of care?

What a priv-i-lege to car-ry Ev-'ry-thing to God in prayer!
We should nev-er be dis-cour-aged, Take it to the Lord in prayer:
Pre-cious Sav-ior, still our ref-uge; Take it to the Lord in prayer:

Oh, what peace we of-ten for-feit, Oh, what need-less pain we bear,
Can we find a friend so faith-ful Who will all our sor-rows share?
Do thy friends de-spise, for-sake thee? Take it to the Lord in prayer;

All be-cause we do not car-ry Ev-'ry-thing to God in prayer!
Je-sus knows our ev-'ry weak-ness, Take it to the Lord in prayer.
In his arms he'll take and shield thee; Thou wilt find a sol-ace there.

Bound by Love

• •

In 1740, in the little hamlet of Lidget Green, Yorkshire, England, a son was born to the Fawcett family. Although poor as the world judges, young John Fawcett was given the riches of faith as his parents taught him from the Holy Bible and encouraged him to grow in the knowledge of God. At the age of sixteen, John made a public announcement of his faith in Christ and his determination to one day become a preacher.

Through diligence and much prayer, John's dreams were realized, and at the age of twenty-six, he was ordained a Baptist minister. Shortly after his ordination, young Pastor Fawcett was called to take the pulpit at a small Baptist chapel in the village of Wainsgate in northern England. Traveling there with his new bride, John established a home and ministered faithfully to the needs of the Baptist community in Wainsgate.

The young couple was soon blessed with a family; and as the children grew and the Fawcetts became an integral part of the town, deep friendships were forged. The material needs of the family grew as well, however, and it became clear that a move to a larger and more prosperous church would benefit the family in many ways. John set about applying for pastorates in other areas of England and was delighted and a bit overwhelmed when the call came from a large church in London. John was to move to the influential Carter's Lane Baptist Church to succeed the well-known Dr. Gill. It was an answer to prayer for the thirty-two-year-old Fawcett, and the future looked promising as he and his little family prepared to make the move south.

In the weeks before his departure, John continued to serve his small congregation as he had for the past six years. Daily, the townspeople streamed to his cottage to offer their thanks, relay their sorrow at his impending departure, and seek some last bits of wisdom from the young pastor they had come to love so dearly.

Finally, the day of departure arrived. John Fawcett had preached his final sermon at Wainsgate, said his final good-byes, and loaded the family's belongings into a horse-drawn wagon. As he and his wife and children boarded the wagon, the members of his church gathered around to pray with their pastor one last time. As the "Amen" was said, John and his wife looked around at the tear-stained faces of their friends and neighbors. Mrs. Fawcett gripped her husband's hand and wept. So moved was he by the deep love of his parishioners, that at that moment, John made a life-changing decision. He jumped down from the wagon seat, went back inside the house, and gave the order to unload his household goods. The Fawcetts would not leave the little Baptist Church of Wainsgate.

The following Sunday, John Fawcett preached from the New Testament Book of Luke, chapter 12, verse 15, which says: "Take heed, and beware of covetousness: for a man's life consisteth not in the abundance of things which he possesseth." At the close of the sermon, Pastor Fawcett read a poem he had composed, entitled "Brotherly Love." Years later the verses were set to music to become the well-loved and familiar hymn, "Blest Be the Tie that Binds."

John Fawcett's determination to remain at Wainsgate was not a passing fancy. Despite a salary that never exceeded $200 per year, and a call to become the President of the prestigious Bristol Baptist Academy, the country pastor remained faithful to his little flock. From his cottage he wrote several books, became well-known for his Biblical scholarship, and even started a school for preachers. But it is likely that he is best remembered and loved for the example he set in his willingness to sacrifice ambition and personal gain for Christian devotion to the fellow pilgrims of his home church.

Blest Be the Tie That Binds

John Fawcett

Johann G. Nageli

1. Blest be the tie that binds Our hearts in Chris-tian love;
2. Be - fore our Fa - ther's throne We pour our ar - dent pray'rs;
3. We share our mu - tual woes, Our mu - tual bur - dens bear;
4. When we a - sun - der part, It gives us in - ward pain;

The fel - low-ship of kin-dred minds Is like to that a - bove.
Our fears, our hopes, our aims are one, Our comforts and our cares.
And of - ten for each oth - er flows The sym-pa - thiz-ing tear.
But we shall still be joined in heart, And hope to meet a - gain. A-men.

HYMNS OF CELEBRATION

A Christmas Eve Blessing

The little town of Oberndorf, Austria, consisted of one winding street lined with quaint cottages and shops when young Josef Mohr arrived in 1818 to take the position of assistant priest at the newly-erected Church of St. Nicholas. Serving in this parish high in the Tyrolean Alps, Father Mohr soon made dear friends among the local villagers. A favorite acquaintance was Franz Gruber, the village schoolmaster and church organist. Together, these two young men spent much time discussing matters of mutual interest, such as education, theology, and music. As Advent approached that year, the two friends lamented the fact that no one had yet been able to compose "the perfect Christmas hymn."

As was the custom in the Alpine mountain villages, a group of traveling players arrived in Oberndorf just before Christmas. Their plan was to present a Nativity play in the local Catholic church. Unfortunately, the organ at the Church of St. Nicholas was being repaired and the church could not be used for their performance that year. A local shop owner generously opened his home to the players, however, and the play was presented, as planned, on the evening of December twenty-third.

Josef Mohr was in attendance that evening. After the performance, moved by the beauty and simplicity of the pageant, the young priest stopped on his way home at a favorite viewpoint overlooking the small village of Oberndorf. There, under the sparkling winter stars, Mohr was moved by the beauty of the night and the inspiration of the Christmas story. Returning home, he lit his lamp and, in its soft glow, wrote the beautiful words of "Silent Night, Holy Night." The next morning, Mohr took his three stanzas of six lines each to the home of his friend, Franz Gruber, and said, "See if you can wed these words to a melody." Reading through the simple verses, Gruber is reported to have replied, "Friend Mohr, you have found it—the right song—God be praised."

Because there was no hope of the organ being repaired in time for the Midnight Mass that Christmas Eve, Gruber wrote the music for guitar. When the congregation was gathered for the services that evening, Mohr sang the tenor part. Gruber sang the bass and played the accompaniment on his guitar while a choir of young girls from the village repeated the last two lines of each stanza in four-part harmony. The Church of St. Nicholas seemed alive with the beauty of the first Christmas as the clear, pure strains of the original hymn filled the night.

Father Mohr and Schoolmaster Gruber had never intended for their carol to become famous, but when the organ builder returned after the holidays to complete his repairs, he heard the song being sung. Enchanted by both verse and melody, he obtained a copy and took it with him when he returned to his home in Zillertal, about eight miles away. Soon the lovely Christmas hymn was being included in concerts throughout Austria and Germany, billed as a Tyrolean Folk Song of unknown origin.

In 1839, "Silent Night, Holy Night" was first performed in the United States by a visiting group of Austrian singers. Before long, it was translated not only into English, but into several other languages as well. Without a doubt, it has become the best-loved Christmas carol of all time. Unknowingly, its author and composer had fulfilled their dream of discovering "the perfect Christmas hymn."

Hymns of Celebration

Silent Night, Holy Night

JOSEPH MOHR

FRANZ GRUBER

A Pastor's Gift to the Children

P hillips Brooks, author of "O Little Town of Bethlehem," was an American preacher, pastor, and teacher of outstanding ability and power. Born in Boston on December 13, 1835, Brooks showed an early interest in the things of the church, especially the hymns sung each week at services. By the time he entered college, he had memorized all the verses to over 200 hymns. After he finished his training for the ministry and began preaching, he often used quotations from these hymns in his sermons.

After receiving a degree from Harvard, Brooks entered the Episcopal Theological Seminary at Alexandria, Virginia. In 1859, at the age of twenty-four, Brooks was ordained in the Episcopal church. His first pastorate was as rector of Holy Trinity Church in Philadelphia. After faithfully serving there for six years, Brooks was given a trip to the Holy Land by his parishioners.

For almost a year, Rev. Brooks retraced the steps of Jesus and the Apostles. On Sunday, December 24, 1865, the young Episcopalian pastor rode on horseback from Jerusalem to Bethlehem and was present at the Christmas Eve service held in Constantine's ancient basilica, built over the traditional site of the nativity. During the services, which lasted from ten o'clock at night until three in the morning, Brooks was moved with emotion as he listened to hymns of praise, Scripture readings, and prayers. The impressions of this Christmas Eve in Bethlehem would remain with him throughout his life

and, just a few years later, would become the backdrop for his beloved Christmas carol.

Returning to Philadelphia, Phillips Brooks again took up his responsibilities as pastor at Holy Trinity. Standing over six-and-a-half feet tall, he was an imposing figure as he worked and taught around the parish. Despite his size and the fact that he was a bachelor, however, Brooks was adored by the children of the church and he seemed to return their affection. On many occasions, parishioners passing by the open door of his study would spy Brooks sitting on the floor surrounded by toys, playing with the children from his Sunday school classes.

It was this love for little ones that led him to write the hauntingly lovely Christmas carol, "O Little Town of Bethlehem." The children of the church were planning a Christmas program and the Reverend wanted a new Christmas song for the children to sing. As he pondered the nativity story, his thoughts drifted back to his Christmas in Bethlehem just a few years earlier. He recalled the beauty of the city, the darkness of the night, the pageantry of the story, and taking pen and paper, he wrote the four stanzas of the poem.

In the morning, Brooks gave the verses to the church organist, Lewis H. Redner, requesting that he compose a simple melody that the children could easily memorize and sing in the Christmas program a few days later. Redner was an accomplished organist and loved composing music; but try as he might, he could not come up with a satisfactory melody for Brooks' poem. On the night before the children were to present their program, Redner fell into bed exhausted, still without the requested tune. In the middle of the night, however, he was awakened suddenly with the strains of a lovely melody ringing in his ears. Hastily, he jotted down the notes, set them by his bedside, and went back to sleep. In the morning he completed the harmony for the inspired tune and taught it to the children. That night in December of 1868, "O Little Town of Bethlehem" was sung for the first time by the children of Holy Trinity Church.

Phillips Brooks moved on the following year to become the pastor of Trinity Church in Boston, where he served from 1869 until 1891. Subsequent to that, he was appointed as the Episcopal Bishop to all the churches in Massachusetts. In all his years of service he was honored and loved by those to whom he ministered, and when the news of his unexpected death reached his parishioners, one little girl was heard to remark: "Oh, Mama, how happy the angels will be!"

Although a beautiful monument stands at Trinity Church in Boston honoring this man of God, one suspects his memory is even more blessed each year at Christmastime when millions of Christians across the world raise their voices to sing his beautiful hymn, "O Little Town of Bethlehem."

O Little Town of Bethlehem

PHILLIPS BROOKS   LEWIS REDNER

A Joyful Collaboration

$\cdots\cdots\cdots\cdots\cdots\cdots\cdots\cdots\cdots\cdots\cdots\cdots$

This favorite Christmas carol was first published in a collection of hymns by the English poet and hymn writer Isaac Watts. The collection, *Psalms of David Imitated in the Language of the New Testament*, was published in 1719 and contained 132 of the 150 psalms from the Bible, interpreted by Watts. "Joy to the World" comes from a paraphrase of Psalm ninety-eight, verses four through nine:

> Make a joyful noise unto the Lord, all
> the earth: make a loud noise,
> and rejoice, and sing praise.
> Sing unto the Lord with the harp;
> with the harp, and voice of a psalm.
> With trumpets and sounds of cornets
> make a joyful noise before the
> Lord, the King.
> Let the sea roar, and the fulness thereof;
> the world, and they that dwell therein.
> Let the floods clap their hands: let the
> hills be joyful together
> before the Lord;
> For he cometh to judge the earth: with
> righteousness shall he judge the world,
> and the peoples with equity.

Isaac Watts was a lover of language and poetry from the time he could first speak. He learned Latin and Greek before the age of nine and by the time he had turned thirteen he was mastering French and Hebrew. He had a brilliant mind and authored several books on religion and philosophy that had a major impact upon English thought during the late seventeenth and early eighteenth centuries.

Despite his deeply intellectual pursuits, Watts had an intense desire to elevate singing in English congregations. He wanted to make the Scriptures relevant to lay people and saw hymns as a perfect vehicle for this. At his father's urging he began, at the age of eighteen, to compose hymns for his own church at the rate of one per week. In 1707 he published 210 of these original hymns in a book entitled, *Hymns and Spiritual Songs*. Throughout his lifetime, in addition to his theological books, Isaac Watts published over 600 hymns, many of which are still popular today. Some of these are: "O God, Our Help in Ages Past," "I Sing the Mighty Power of God," "Jesus Shall Reign," "When I Survey the Wondrous Cross," "Am I a Soldier of the Cross?" "At the Cross," and "Marching to Zion."

Still, however beautiful the words Isaac Watts wrote in paraphrasing the ninety-eighth Psalm, "Joy to the World" would not have become the popular Christmas favorite it is without the contributions of two other important men. It is interesting that these two men were from opposite sides of the Atlantic, lived in different centuries, and never met; yet their collaboration provided the majestic melody for "Joy to the World."

The first, George Frederick Handel, was a German-born prodigy who by the age of twelve had mastered the violin, oboe, harpsichord, and organ while studying law at the university! At thirteen, he decided to give up his legal studies to devote his life to music. After spending several years in Hamburg composing operas, Handel traveled throughout Italy performing his compositions. In 1712 he made his second trip to England and shortly after that, decided to become an English citizen. When the popularity of grand opera began to wane, Handel turned to composing oratorios. His famous oratorio, "The Messiah," was written during this time, in the unbelievably short period of just twenty-four days. It was first performed in Dublin, Ireland on April 13, 1742.

The second composer to have a vital part in bringing "Joy to the World" to us was the American choir director and educator, Lowell Mason. Mason was no stranger to hymns, having hundreds of compositions to his credit during his long and fruitful life. It was his custom to search through previously published hymn texts to find material for his original melodies. Perhaps this is how he came upon Isaac Watts' interpretation of the ninety-eighth Psalm. In an effort to find a suitable melody that conveyed the joyous message of the words, Mason turned to Handel's "Messiah." Taking musical phrases from different sections of the oratorio, Mason arranged them into a tune he called "Antioch." Wedded to the words of Isaac Watts, Mason's uplifting melody was published for the first time in 1836.

Three very different men from three very different backgrounds united their hearts and minds to produce this beautiful Christmas carol that has lifted spirits heavenward for over 150 Christmases. Their joint inspiration has truly brought joy to the world!

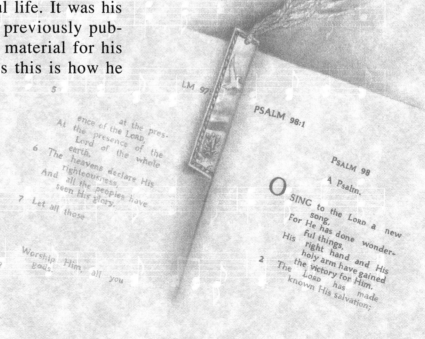

Joy to the World!

Isaac Watts

ARR. BY LOWELL MASON
GEORGE FREDERICK HANDEL

1. Joy to the world! the Lord is come; Let earth re-ceive her King;
2. Joy to the earth! the Sav-ior reigns; Let men their songs em-ploy;
3. No more let sins and sor-rows grow, Nor thorns in-fest the ground;
4. He rules the world with truth and grace, And makes the na-tions prove

Let ev-'ry heart pre-pare him room,
While fields and floods, rocks, hills, and plains
He comes to make his bless-ings flow
The glo-ries of his righ-teous-ness,

And heav'n and na-ture sing, And heav'n and na-ture sing,
Re-peat the sound-ing joy, Re-peat the sound-ing joy,
Far as the curse is found, Far as the curse is found,
And won-ders of his love, And won-ders of his love,

1. And heav'n and na-ture sing,

1. And heav'n and na-ture sing, And heav'n and na-

And heav'n, and heav'n and na-ture sing.
Re-peat, re-peat the sound-ing joy.
Far as, far as the curse is found.
And won-ders, won-ders of his love.

ture sing,

HYMNS OF TRIUMPH

Rallying Cry of the Reformation

The years following 1520 were dark and filled with danger for Martin Luther. Despite serving for several years as an Augustinian priest, he had become an adversary of the Catholic church after publicizing his objections to the practice of selling indulgences. Eventually, Luther was excommunicated for this position, and his public declarations and criticism placed him at the center of controversy. Threatened with arrest and extradition to Rome for trial, Luther was placed in protective custody by a sympathetic German official. The ex-priest was locked in a castle near Eisenach, Germany for over a year.

Never one to waste time, Luther used this forced isolation for a project he had been wanting to accomplish, and began his translation of the Bible from Greek into German. He felt strongly that the people ought to be able to read the Holy Scriptures in their own language and also to speak directly to God through hymns in their native tongue. To this end, he composed a hymn book for use by German congregations. With the translation of the New Testament into German in 1522, the publication of a hymn book in 1524, and the completion of the Old Testament translation in 1534, Luther provided the foundation for the Protestant Reformation in Germany. In his honor, German Protestants became known as Lutherans.

If there was a theme song of the Reformation it would have to be Luther's powerful hymn, "A Mighty Fortress Is Our God." Based on the first verse of Psalm forty-six, "God is our refuge and strength," this hymn became the rallying cry of peasants and dissidents across Europe. Its inspiring verses were on the lips of Protestant emigres on their way to exile, armies as they went into battle, and even Protestant martyrs as they went to their deaths. It has been translated into almost every known language, and is today the national hymn of Germany.

Martin Luther knew the power of congregational singing and saw it as a powerful tool for bringing men and women closer to God. He wrote: "If any man despises music, as all fanatics do, for him I have no liking; for music is a gift and grace of God, not an invention of men. Thus it drives out the devil and makes people cheerful. Then one forgets all wrath, impurity, and other devices."

After being cast out of the Catholic church, Luther married a former nun, Katherine von Bora, in 1525. Together they continued to work tirelessly for the cause of the Reformation. When he died in 1546, in his hometown of Eisleben, Germany, Luther had, through his theological writings, his Bible translations, and through his hymns, laid the foundations of a movement that would forever change the religious history of the world. In recognition of this, "A Mighty Fortress Is Our God" was sung at his funeral and the first line of the hymn is inscribed on his tomb in Eisleben.

A Mighty Fortress Is Our God

MARTIN LUTHER   MARTIN LUTHER

A Teacher's Tribute

In the summer of 1893, Katharine Lee Bates stood atop Pike's Peak in Colorado. She had been traveling throughout the summer from her home in Massachusetts across the United States, enjoying the sights, both man-made and natural. Earlier, in Chicago, she had visited the Columbia Exposition and had seen a beautiful model city, crafted of white stone to depict the architect's vision of the cities of tomorrow. It was the year of the 400th anniversary of the discovery of America and now, as Katharine Bates stood on the windy mountain summit, the experiences of the past few weeks seemed to come together in a vision of her beloved country.

She could see the purple haze clinging to the majestic Rocky Mountains. The fruitful Colorado plains stretched in the distance, and beyond them the grain fields of Kansas and Nebraska. In her memoirs she wrote: "It was there, as I was looking out over the sea-like expanse of fertile country spreading away so far under the ample skies, that the opening lines of this text formed themselves in my mind."

Returning to her hotel room, she sat down to compose the lines of the patriotic hymn we now know as "America the Beautiful." As she considered the natural beauty and wonders of this country, her thoughts were drawn also to the kinds of people whose determination and sacrifices carved a nation from the land. The pilgrims of her hymn were not just those men and women who landed at Plymouth Rock, but the countless others whose feet had tramped the paths and trails across the plains, rivers, deserts, and mountains to expand the nation's boundaries.

And in the final verse, her thoughts seem drawn back to the vision of the future she witnessed in Chicago. In fact, she wrote later: "The White City made such a strong appeal to the patriotic feeling that it was in no small degree responsible for at least the last stanza of 'America the Beautiful.' It was with this quickened and deepened sense of America that I went on, my New England eyes delighting in the wind-waved gold of the vast wheat fields."

Far from being a sentimental bit of patriotic poetry that ignores the flaws of her native land, Bates' verses include the recognition that America needs the hand of God to guide her to greatness. She makes a plea for brotherhood, self-control, mercy, and nobleness—qualities of the spirit that will match the majesty of the natural beauty this country offers.

Miss Bates was no stranger to the literary world, having taught English at Wellesley College before becoming the head of the English department there. She did not consider her poem, "America the Beautiful," for publication, however, until about ten years later when she simplified the phrasing and submitted it to the editor of the *Boston Evening Transcript*. He recognized the value of the poem and published it on November 19, 1904.

Although greeted with enthusiasm as a poem, Miss Bates' stirring verses were not set to music for many more years. Several editors of hymn books searched for a melody that would blend well with the patriotic stanzas and dozens were tried without success. Finally, a melody composed ten years before the text was discovered in the writings of Samuel Ward, a New Jersey businessman. Ward had died, however, and permission to use the melody needed to be granted by his widow. By 1912, such permission was given, and "America the Beautiful" was published in its present form.

Even with the stirring melody and words finally together, the hymn did not become instantly popular. It took the darkest days of World War I to bring that about. With the war raging, "America the Beautiful" became a song that bonded a weary nation together with a vision of hope and peaceful prosperity. It gave a musical testimony to the national motto, "One nation under God."

Recently, it has been suggested by some that "America the Beautiful" be adopted as our country's national anthem. Although it is doubtful that it will ever replace "The Star Spangled Banner," one cannot deny that it has become our country's national hymn.

America the Beautiful

KATHERINE LEE BATES

SAMUEL A. WARD

1. O beau-ti-ful for spa-cious skies, For am-ber waves of grain,
2. O beau-ti-ful for pil-grim feet, Whose stern, im-pas-sioned stress
3. O beau-ti-ful for he-roes proved In lib-er-at-ing strife,
4. O beau-ti-ful for pa-triot dream That sees, be-yond the years,

For pur-ple moun-tain maj-es-ties A-bove the fruit-ed plain!
A thor-ough-fare for free-dom beat A-cross the wil-der-ness!
Who more than self their coun-try loved, And mer-cy more than life!
Thine al-a-bas-ter cit-ies gleam, Un-dimmed by hu-man tears!

A-mer-i-ca! A-mer-i-ca! God shed his grace on thee,
A-mer-i-ca! A-mer-i-ca! God mend thine ev-'ry flaw,
A-mer-i-ca! A-mer-i-ca! May God thy gold re-fine,
A-mer-i-ca! A-mer-i-ca! God shed his grace on thee,

And crown thy good with broth-er-hood From sea to shin-ing sea.
Con-firm thy soul in self-con-trol, Thy lib-er-ty in law.
Till all suc-cess be no-ble-ness, And ev-'ry gain di-vine.
And crown thy good with broth-er-hood From sea to shin-ing sea.

Hymns of Triumph

A Suffragette's Song for Soldiers

The year was 1861 and the battle lines were being drawn as the opposing sides, North and South, prepared for war. Day after day, troops marched through the streets of the nation's capital; some in trim blue uniforms with polished leather and shining swords, others in worn out work clothes, carrying rusty rifles. As they marched past Julia Ward Howe's open windows, she could hear them whistling or singing in unison. They were young and inexperienced in the agonies of war and that made their raucous singing all the more tragic.

One of their favorite tunes seemed to be "John Brown's Body," a grim ditty about the hanging of a militant abolitionist. The tune was catchy and easily sung, but the words were depressing and morose. As Julia stood watching a parade of Union soldiers pass by one day, she was joined by a visiting friend from Boston, Rev. James Freeman Clarke. He remarked on the song they were singing, the ever popular "John Brown's Body," and suggested that it would be a good song if someone would just write some decent words to go with the tune. Knowing that Julia had a gift for poetry and that she had already published two volumes of her own works, he put the challenge to her. Although the thought hadn't occurred to her previously, it seemed a good idea and Julia accepted the task.

She returned home that evening with the melody running through her mind, but being exhausted from the day's activities, she went to bed without beginning to work on the verses. She fell into a peaceful sleep, but awoke before dawn with the beginnings of a poem growing in her mind. She was afraid that if she lay there any longer, the thoughts would flee; so, as she reports in her journal, "I sprang out of bed and in the dimness found an old stump of a pen, which I remembered using the day before. I scrawled the verses almost without looking at the paper."

The following day she shared her composition with Rev. Clarke as well as some others and her "Battle Hymn of the Republic" was received with enthusiasm. They urged her to submit the poem for publication and, in February of 1862, Julia Ward Howe's poem was published in *The Atlantic Monthly*. The author received a check for the sum of five dollars from the magazine.

It was not long before the whole nation was singing Julia Howe's stirring hymn. President Lincoln was said to have been moved to tears almost every time the majestic chorus "Glory! Glory! Hallelujah!" was sung at a public gathering and this, more than any other hymn, became identified with his war-torn presidency.

Union prisoners held in the infamous Confederate Libby Prison at Richmond, Virginia, made it their defiant and hope-filled anthem. The patriotic and inspiring tone of the "Battle Hymn of the Republic" is not solely American, however; men and women in other countries have also been uplifted by its victorious chorus. In 1965, at the state funeral of Sir Winston Churchill, the band played "The Battle Hymn of the Republic."

Julia Ward Howe's contributions to the life of her country were not limited to poetry. She was active in both political and religious movements in the late nineteenth and early twentieth centuries. Joining a group called the Radical Club, she became a student of modern philosophies and an active member of the Unitarian church, where she frequently delivered sermons on a variety of liberal causes. Besides being very outspoken about her opposition to slavery and speaking out against it at every opportunity, Julia was a leader in the Women's Suffrage Movement. In addition to these involvements, she was instrumental in organizing an international crusade in 1870 calling for all women of the world to unite for the purpose of ending war for all time.

When she died in 1910 at the age of ninety-one, Julia Ward Howe left a country much different from the one she entered almost a century before. Many of the battles for which she fought have been won, and her legacy in poetry and music continues to inspire citizens to defend the way of truth. She gave her country a marching song and her words still challenge us today.

Battle Hymn of the Republic

JULIA WARD HOWE

AMERICAN FOLK SONG

1. Mine eyes have seen the glo-ry of the com-ing of the Lord;
2. I have seen him in the watch-fires of a hun-dred cir-cling camps;
3. He has sound-ed forth the trum-pet that shall nev-er sound re-treat;
4. In the beau-ty of the lil-ies, Christ was born a-cross the sea,
5. He is com-ing like the glo-ry of the morn-ing on the wave;

He is tram-pling out the vin-tage where the grapes of wrath are stored;
They have build-ed him an al-tar in the eve-ning dews and damps;
He is sift-ing out the hearts of men be-fore his judg-ment seat;
With a glo-ry in his bos-om that trans-fig-ures you and me;
He is wis-dom to the might-y, he is hon-or to the brave;

He hath loosed the fate-ful light-ning of his ter-ri-ble swift sword;
I can read his right-eous sen-tence by the dim and flar-ing lamps;
O be swift, my soul, to an-swer him; be ju-bi-lant, my feet!
As he died to make men ho-ly, let us live to make men free,
So the world shall be his foot-stool, and the soul of wrong his slave.

His truth is march-ing on.
His day is march-ing on.
Our God is march-ing on. Glo-ry! glo-ry, hal-le-lu-jah! Glo-ry!
While God is march-ing on.
Our God is march-ing on.

glo-ry, hal-le-lu-jah! Glo-ry! glo-ry, hal-le-lu-jah! Our God is marching on.

155

Hymns of Triumph

A March for All Ages

· ·

Sabine Baring-Gould was the new Anglican curate in the parish at Horbury Bridge in Yorkshire, England, in 1864. Time was nearing for the annual Whitmonday procession of Sunday school children from one village to the next, and Baring-Gould despaired of keeping his little charges in line as they tramped over the countryside. As he considered the problem, it came to mind that a marching tune would be appropriate to help keep the children in step and all headed in the same direction—physically as well as spiritually!

The young curate reviewed his hymn texts, but could find nothing he felt was appropriate. Undaunted by the problem, he sat up that evening and composed the verses of "Onward Christian Soldiers." In his own account of the writing of his hymn, Baring-Gould has said: "It was written in a very simple fashion, without thought of publication. It was written in great haste, and I am afraid that some of the rhymes are faulty. I am certain that nothing has surprised me more than its popularity."

Although this hastily written children's song is the one piece of writing for which Sabine Baring-Gould is most remembered, it is interesting to note that he was one of the most gifted men-of-letters of the Victorian era. During his lifetime he wrote eighty-five books on religion, travel, folklore, mythology, history, fiction, biography, and theology. One of his best known publications is his fif-teen-volume *Lives of the Saints*. In the British Museum's literary catalogue there are more titles by Baring-Gould than by any other writer of his time!

When it was first performed by the children of Baring-Gould's Sunday school, "Onward Christian Soldiers" was sung to a melody by Haydn. The hymn did not gain its great popularity, however, until a second melody was composed for it by Arthur Seymour Sullivan, a man well-known for the operettas he wrote in collaboration with the English librettist, W.S. Gilbert. When Baring-Gould's poetry was joined with Sullivan's stirring marching tune, "Onward Christian Soldiers" became a favorite with congregations across Great Britain and America.

The inspiring combination of words and music has uplifted hearts on more than one momentous occasion. When Franklin Roosevelt and Winston Churchill met on the deck of the British battleship *Prince of Wales* for the signing of the Atlantic Charter on August 10, 1941, each leader chose hymns to be sung at the Sunday morning services. Churchill selected "Onward Christian Soldiers" and later said in a British radio broadcast: "We sang 'Onward Christian Soldiers,' and indeed, I felt that this was no vain presumption by that we had the right to feel that we were serving a cause for the sake of which a trumpet has sounded from on high." As the two countries united on that historic day to oppose Hitler in World War II, this stirring hymn focused their attention not only on their goals, but also on their motives.

When he died in 1924, at the age of ninety, Sabine Baring-Gould left the literary world greatly enriched by his numerous contributions. And with his hastily written children's song, he also enriched the world of Christian music. He has given believers everywhere a cadence for commitment and a challenge to march on as soldiers for Christ.

Onward Christian Soldiers

Sabine Baring-Gould

Arthur S. Sullivan

1. On-ward, Chris-tian sol-diers, Marching as to war, With the cross of Je-sus Go-ing on be-fore! Christ, the roy-al Mas-ter, Leads a-gainst the foe; For-ward in-to bat-tle, See his ban-ner go!

2. At the sign of tri-umph Sa-tan's host doth flee; On, then, Chris-tian sol-diers, On to vic-to-ry! Hell's foun-da-tions quiv-er At the shout of praise; Broth-ers, lift your voic-es, Loud your anthems raise!

3. Like a might-y ar-my Moves the church of God; Broth-ers, we are tread-ing Where the saints have trod; We are not di-vid-ed; All one bod-y we, One in hope and doc-trine, One in char-i-ty.

4. On-ward, then, ye peo-ple, Join our hap-py throng, Blend with ours your voic-es In the tri-umph song; Glo-ry, laud, and hon-or, Un-to Christ the King; This thro' countless a-ges Men and an-gels sing.

On-ward, Chris-tian sol-diers, March-ing as to war, With the cross of Je-sus Go-ing on be-fore!

Hymn Index

Project Editor, Nancy J. Skarmeas; **Associate Editor**, D. Fran Morley; **Permissions Editor**, Kathleen Gilbert; **Book Designer**, Patrick McRae; **Pencil Drawings**, Tim Peterson

Photography Credits

3 Evening Devotions, Gerald Koser. **7** Crown of Thorns, Alice & Frank Rodziewicz. **10** Moody Scenic, Freelance Photo Guild. **14** National Cathedral, H. Armstrong Roberts. **19** North Rim, Grand Canyon National Park from Point Imperial, Dick Dietrich. **22** Hope River, South Island, New Zealand, Tom Till. **30** White Church in Autumn, Fred Dole. **34** Olympic National Park from Hurricane Ridge, Washington, Dick Dietrich. **38** Last Rays of Sunlight, Hawaii, Dick Dietrich. **43** Rolling Surf, Ken Dequaine. **47** Sun through Trees, Freelance Photo Guild. **51** Zion National Park, Utah, Bob Clemenz. **55** Goat Beach, Sonoma Coastline, Jenner, California, Ed Cooper. **59** Organ Pipes, Speyer, Germany, H. Armstrong Roberts. **62** Swan, Comstock Photography. **67** Rose Window, Washington Cathedral, Washington, D.C., Fred Sieb. **70** Giant Sequoias, Grant Grove, Kings Canyon National Park, California, Ed Cooper. **75** Stained Glass Crucifix, Dick Dietrich. **79** Easter Lilies, Fred Sieb. **83** Proxy Falls, McKenzie Pass, Oregon, Bob Clemenz. **87** Sweetpeas and Butterfly, Monserratte Schwartz. **91** Cross, Robert Cushman Hayes. **94** Oregon Coast, Dick Dietrich. **99** Roses with Dew, Adam Jones. **103** Fall Pond, Dave Conley, The Stock Solution. **106** Blanket Flower, Ringwood, New Jersey, Gene Ahrens. **111** Trumpet and Lilies, H. Armstrong Roberts. **114** Purple Irises, Michael Magnuson. **118** Air Force Chapel, Ed Cooper. **123** First Flower, Ray Elliot, Jr. **126** The Good Shepherd, Gary Blodgett. **131** Waterlilies, Itasca State Park, Minnesota, Tom Till. **134** Winter Doorway, H. Armstrong Roberts. **148** Mt. Rainier National Park, Washington, Ed Cooper. **142** Rose Window, Universal Media. **147** Banff National Park, Alberta, Canada, Bob Clemenz. **150** Mt. Shuksan, Washington, Bob Clemenz. **154** Rustic Cabin, Gene Ahrens. **158** Walkway Beauty, Gottlieb Hampfler, H. Armstrong Roberts.